Business Analytics
for Managers

Wiley & SAS Business Series

The Wiley & SAS Business Series presents books that help senior-level managers with their critical management decisions.

Titles in the Wiley and SAS Business Series include:

Activity-Based Management for Financial Institutions: Driving Bottom-Line Results by Brent Bahnub

Business Intelligence Competency Centers: A Team Approach to Maximizing Competitive Advantage by Gloria J. Miller, Dagmar Brautigam, and Stefanie Gerlach

Business Intelligence Success Factors: Tools for Aligning Your Business in the Global Economy by Olivia Parr Rud

Case Studies in Performance Management: A Guide from the Experts by Tony C. Adkins

CIO Best Practices: Enabling Strategic Value with Information Technology by Joe Stenzel

Credit Risk Assessment: The New Lending System for Borrowers, Lenders, and Investors by Clark Abrahams and Mingyuan Zhang

Credit Risk Scorecards: Developing and Implementing Intelligent Credit Scoring by Naeem Siddiqi

Customer Data Integration: Reaching a Single Version of the Truth by Jill Dyche and Evan Levy

Demand-Driven Forecasting: A Structured Approach to Forecasting by Charles Chase

Enterprise Risk Management: A Methodology for Achieving Strategic Objectives by Gregory Monahan

Fair Lending Compliance: Intelligence and Implications for Credit Risk Management by Clark R. Abrahams and Mingyuan Zhang

Information Revolution: Using the Information Evolution Model to Grow Your Business by Jim Davis, Gloria J. Miller, and Allan Russell

Marketing Automation: Practical Steps to More Effective Direct Marketing by Jeff LeSueur

Mastering Organizational Knowledge Flow: How to Make Knowledge Sharing Work by Frank Leistner

Performance Management: Finding the Missing Pieces (to Close the Intelligence Gap) by Gary Cokins

Performance Management: Integrating Strategy Execution, Methodologies, Risk, and Analytics by Gary Cokins

The Business Forecasting Deal: Exposing Bad Practices and Providing Practical Solutions by Michael Gilliland

The Data Asset: How Smart Companies Govern Their Data for Business Success by Tony Fisher

The New Know: Innovation Powered by Analytics by Thornton May

Visual Six Sigma: Making Data Analysis Lean by Ian Cox, Marie A. Gaudard, Philip J. Ramsey, Mia L. Stephens, and Leo Wright

For more information on any of the above titles, please visit www.wiley.com.

Business Analytics for Managers

*Taking Business
Intelligence beyond Reporting*

**Gert H.N. Laursen
Jesper Thorlund**

WILEY

John Wiley & Sons, Inc.

Published by John Wiley & Sons, Inc., Hoboken, New Jersey.
Published simultaneously in Canada.

For general information on our other products and services or for technical support, please contact our Customer Care Department within the United States at (800) 762-2974, outside the United States at (317) 572-3993 or fax (317) 572-4002.

Wiley also publishes its books in a variety of electronic formats. Some content that appears in print may not be available in electronic books. For more information about Wiley products, visit our web site at www.wiley.com.

Library of Congress Cataloging-in-Publication Data
Laursen, Gert H. N.
  Business analytics for managers: taking business intelligence beyond reporting/ Gert H.N. Laursen, Jesper Thorlund.
    p. cm. – (Wiley and SAS business series)
  Includes index.
  ISBN 978-0-470-89061-5 (hardback)
    1. Business intelligence. I. Thorlund, Jesper. II. Title.
  HD38.7.L39 2010
  658.4'09033–dc22

                                                                    2010016217

Printed in the United States of America

10 9 8 7 6 5 4

Contents

Foreword

This book is more fuel for this era of strategic and unified views of business analytics for value creation. In the same vein as *Competing on Analytics* and *Analytics at Work*, *Business Analytics for Managers: Business Intelligence beyond Reporting* adds another interesting and worthwhile perspective on the topic. In times of rapid change and growing complexity, rapid learning becomes more valuable. This book provides the strategic view on what's required to enable rapid learning and ultimately value creation.

How we make decisions using huge, noisy, messy data requires business analytics. True appreciation and advocacy for the analytical perspective on the whole of business analytics is important—an analytical perspective on data (as a strategic asset), on methods and processes (to be refined and optimized), on people (the diverse skills it takes to formulate and execute on a well-thought-through strategy).

It starts with an analytical view of data—what are you measuring and are you measuring what matters? Measurement (data generation and collection) is itself a process—the process of manufacturing an asset. When data is viewed this way, the analytical concepts of quality improvement and process optimization can be applied. The authors essentially ask "What are you doing with your data? How are people in your organization armed to make better decisions using the data, processes, and analytical methods available?"

Business analytics as portrayed by these analytical thinkers is about value creation. Value creation can take different forms through greater efficiency or greater effectiveness. Better decisions to reduce costs, reveal opportunity, and better allocate resources can all create value. The authors provide valuable business analytics foundational concepts to help organizations create value in a sustainable and scalable way.

Why business analytics? Even though some have tried to expand the definition of the relatively aged term, *business intelligence*, there is no real consistency, so a new term reflecting a new focus is warranted. Further, through promotion of a process view, we break out of some of the silothink and see the importance of closing the loop—on data (data quality and measuring what matters), on process (to continuously learn and improve), and on performance (to make the best decisions, enable the best actions, and measure impact). How many organizations continue producing text-heavy, tabular reports reporting on old and perhaps out-of-date metrics that few take the time to consume? How old are some of the processes driving key decisions in organizations? What opportunity costs are you incurring and how could you be creating more value?

This book provides a synthesized view of analysis, traditional business intelligence, and performance management, all of which are connected and need to be orchestrated in a strategic way for maximum impact. The chapter advocating a shared strategic resource—a competency center or center of excellence—is an excellent way to drive best practices and create more value, making the case for treating data as a strategic asset and investing in the appropriate analytic infrastructure to maximize value.

Wherever you may be on your business analytics journey, you will find worthwhile thinking, shared expertise, and solid practical advice in this book to help you create more value in a sustainable and scalable way. It is not just analytics as a step in any given business process, but the analytical perspective on any process that is key to understanding what it takes to drive continuous learning and improvement.

Anne Milley
Senior Director of Analytic Strategy
SAS Institute

Introduction

Imagine a company. It could be an American manufacturer of home computers. Try to imagine, too, all the things such a company must be able to do: purchasing from suppliers, assembling and packaging the parts, preparing manuals and marketing plans, selling the products. The company also has a large number of support functions. Someone must look after the well-being of its employees, new staff must be hired, people must be paid, the place must be cleaned, and a canteen must work to feed everyone. We have the entire financial function, ensuring that the crediting and debiting of banks, suppliers, owners, and customers run smoothly. Finally, there are all the planning processes that are related to product lines and to customer groups that the company has chosen to focus on.

Now imagine how much of this the company could outsource. Without too much effort, all production could be moved to the Far East. And, that could probably even bring huge advantages, since it is typically salary-heavy and standardized production work to assemble computers. Others could handle the logistic side of things. You could get professionals to write and translate the manuals. Actually, the company wouldn't even need its own outlets; its products could be sold through some of the major retail chains. Alternatively, a Web shop could be commissioned to create an Internet site, where customers could order the products they want. There is no real need for the company to have its own warehouse for parts and computers, from their arrival to their delivery to the customers. A lot of the support functions could be outsourced, too. Many companies outsource the process of recruiting the right people. Routine tasks such as paying salaries, developing training plans and executing them in external courses could be outsourced, once the company has put these routines in place. Cleaning, the running of the canteen, refilling vending machines, and mowing grass are functions that are already, as a rule, outsourced by large IT companies.

By now, there is not much left of our company. We have removed all the functions that others can do almost as well or, in some cases, even better. What we have left is what we call the company's core competencies. These competencies include things the company is especially good at, and which can secure its survival in the future, provided it is capable of developing these so that they continue to meet the requirements in the marketplace.

As shown in our example, core competencies have little to do with the physical world. Machinery, warehouses, and distribution can be outsourced. A company's core competencies lie in the field of knowing how to handle internal processes, and knowing what customers want now and in the future. In other words, the key is to have the right knowledge in the company. More specifically, what the company needs is for the right people to have the right data and information at the right time. When that happens, we have rational decision making that meets strategic, operational, and market conditions. And this is exactly how we define business analytics in this book:

> *Delivering the right decision support to the right people at the right time.*

In our definition, we have chosen the term *decision support*, because business analytics gives you, the business user, data, information, or knowledge, which you can choose to act upon or not. Here's a familiar example: An analysis of check-out receipts can inform the manager of a 7-Eleven store which products are often purchased together, thus providing the necessary decision support to guide the placement of goods on the shelves.

This definition seeks to get to the same point as the saying "people don't buy drills; they buy holes" and points out that "people don't buy servers, pivot tables, and algorithms; they buy the ability to monitor and control their business processes along with insights about how to improve them."

Regardless of whether it is predictive models or forecasting, it's the historical information that can give you a status on the situation you are in right now. Maybe your analysts and their scenario models can present you with different alternatives, but ultimately it's the responsibility of the decision makers to choose which business processes they want to alter or initiate based on the decision support. Business analytics is about improving the business's basis for decision making, its operational processes, and the competitiveness obtained when a business is in possession of relevant facts and knows how to use them. In our work as consultants, we have too often experienced business analytics (BA) as purely an IT discipline, primarily driven by the organization's technical environment, which results in BA initiatives floating aimlessly. Successful BA initiatives are always closely interlinked with the organization's strategy (mission, vision, and goals) and are put in place to strengthen the ability of business processes to move in the right direction toward business objectives. Unfortunately, these points are often overlooked, which is one of the reasons for this book.

Business analytics is not a new phenomenon—it's been around for the past 20 years—but with a firm anchoring in the technically oriented environment. Only recently is it making its breakthrough as the business is assuming ownership. We are seeing more and more companies, especially in the financial and the telecom sector, set up actual business analytics departments, designed to support business processes and improve performance. So what is the reason for this shift and the embedding of BA in the organization?

One reason is that decision makers are noticing excellent examples of companies where BA has made a difference.

Here is one example. Euro Disney uses BA to avoid overcrowding of visitors in the amusement park, and to optimize the distribution of its staff. Visitors' activities and movements are predicted and are subject to continuous follow-up in relation to key performance indicators (KPIs). Areas of the amusement park that attract many visitors are swiftly identified and handled by staff, who are moved to these areas from less busy ones. The system has more than 800 points of sale, distributed on 20 different data sources. Data is retrieved from hotels, box-offices, food outlets, shops, and attractions. After the introduction of BA, customer satisfaction is up by 15%, and staff efficiency is up, too. When BA solutions are executed in the right way, money is saved and both customer and employee satisfaction increase.

By now, it's an acknowledged fact that all the money that is invested is returned many-fold when BA solutions are implemented and executed in the right way.

WHAT DOES BA MEAN? INFORMATION SYSTEMS—NOT TECHNICAL SOLUTIONS

It's quite easy to imagine a bank that runs all its customer processes and dialogue programs entirely without using IT—and what really hard work that would be. The point here is, of course, that you can have BA without deploying software and IT solutions. At a basic level, that has been done for centuries, but today, it just wouldn't stack up. In this book, we look at BA as information systems, consisting of three elements:

1. The information systems contain a technological element, which will typically be IT-based, but which in principle could be anything from papyrus scrolls and yellow sticky notes to clever heads with good memories. A characteristic of the technological element is that it can be used to collect, store, and deliver information. In the real world, we're almost always talking about electronic data, which can be collected, merged, and stored for analysts or the so-called front-end systems who will deliver information to end-users. A front-end is the visual presentation of information and data to a user. This can be a sales report in HTML format or graphs in a spreadsheet. A *front-end system* is thus a whole system of visual presentations and data.

2. Human competencies form part of the information systems, too. Someone must be able to retrieve data and deliver it as information in, for instance, a front-end system, and analysts must know how to generate knowledge targeted toward specific decision processes. Even more important, those who make the decisions, those who potentially should change their behavior based on the decision support, are people who must be able to grasp the decision support handed to them.

3. Finally, the information systems must contain some specific business processes that make use of the information or the new knowledge. A business process could be how you optimize inventory or how you price your products. After all, if the organization is not going to make use of the created information, there's no reason to invest in a data warehouse, a central storage facility that combines and optimizes the organization's data for business use.

The considerable investment required to establish a data warehouse must render a positive return for the organization through improved organization-wide decision making. If this doesn't happen, a data warehouse is nothing but a cost that should never have been incurred. An information system is therefore both a facility (for instance a data warehouse, which can store information) as well as competencies that can retrieve and place this information in the right procedural context.

When working with BA, it is therefore not enough to just have an IT technical perspective—that just means seeing the organization as nothing but a *system technical landscape*, where you add another layer. It is essential to look at the organization as a large number of processes. For instance, the primary process in a manufacturing company will typically consist of purchasing raw materials and semi-manufactured products from suppliers, manufacturing the products, storing these and selling them on. In relation to this primary process there are a large number of secondary processes, such as repairing machinery, cleaning, employing and training staff, and so on.

Therefore, when working with BA, it is essential to be able to identify which business processes to support via the information system, as well as to identify how added value is achieved. Finally, it's important to see the company as an accumulation of competencies, and provide the information system with an identification and training of staff, some of whom undertake the technical solution, and others who can bridge the technical and the business-driven side of the organization, with focus on business processes. In terms of added value, this can be achieved in two ways: by an improved deployment of the input resources of the existing process, which means that efficiency increases, or by giving the users of the process added value, which means that what comes out of the process will have increased user or customer satisfaction. We'll discuss this in more detail in Chapter 3.

In other words, successful deployment of BA requires a certain level of abstraction. This is because it's necessary to be able to see the organization as a system technical landscape, an accumulation of competencies as well as a number of processes and, finally, to be able to integrate these three perspectives into each other. To make it all harder, the information systems must be implemented into an organization that perceives itself as a number of departments with different tasks and decision competencies and that occasionally does not even perceive them as being members of the same value chain.

PURPOSE AND AUDIENCE

We have written this guide to business analytics in order to provide:

- A guide to fuel what we refer to as the analytical age, which as the title of the book tells us, is to take business intelligence (BI) beyond reporting. In this book, we will introduce terms like *lead information*, which is the innovative decision support you need in order to revolutionize your processes landscape—typically done via business analytics. This should be seen as opposed to traditional business intelligence producing *lag information* in the form of reports that help users to monitor, maintain, and make evolutionary improvements of their processes. These two types of decision support should be seen as supporting sets of information. However, as shown in Exhibit I.1, the value from a business perspective is different. You can compete on lead information, where lag information to a larger extent is maintaining and optimizing already existing processes.

- The ability to make an information strategy, which basically is a plan of what your BA department should focus on according to your company strategy. After you have read this book, you should have a framework that allows you to make a link

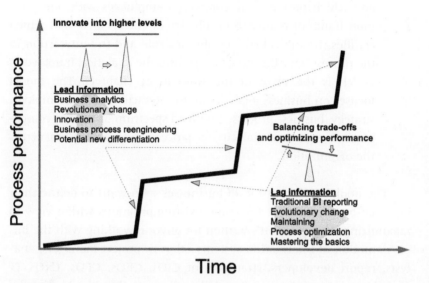

Process development over time

EXHIBIT I.1 The Stairway Chart: Emphasizing the Difference between Lead and Lag Information

between your overall organizational strategy and which specific data you should source in your data warehouse. You need this framework not just for standard reporting, but also to support your company's ability to innovate in the future by using analytics.

- An understanding of BA as a holistic information discipline with links to business's strategy, source data from the operational systems, as well as the entire value chain in between—so not just IT technology. Business anlaytics is a combination of IT technology, human competencies, and organizational processes.

- An understanding of the ever-increasing role of BA, a role which today is aimed at optimizing at business process level but which, we believe, in the near future will be aimed at optimizing individual human behavior as discussed in Chapter 9.

- A reference work containing the most-frequently used business analytics concepts, definitions, and terminology. We have developed a BA model, which gives a helicopter perspective, and which provides the company's employees with one common frame of reference for objectives and means—and which clarifies the individual contributor's role and the interaction in the process. Our BA model constitutes the analytical framework, which is the pivot of the subsequent chapters. The model focuses on business analytics as an interaction of IT technology, strategy, business processes, a broad spectrum of human competencies, organizational circumstances, and cooperation across the organization.

The book is relevant for all businesses who want to define their information strategies or fine-tune existing programs with a view to maximizing their effect. It's written for anyone working with the implementation of information systems—that is, project managers, analysts, report developers, strategists or CIOs, CEOs, CFOs, CxOs, IT professionals, and database specialists. But we should add that the book is of relevance to anyone working operationally with these information systems, since it will highlight the role of these in terms of the overall strategy of the company. Thus, the book is for everyone in business-focused functions in sales, marketing, finance, management, production, and HR who works at a strategic level.

If, for instance, you are working with customer relationship management (CRM), and wish to focus systematically on customer retention via churn analyses, this also requires the involvement of product managers, who, based on the customer profiles to be retained, must develop retention products. Customer service functions, such as call centers, need to be integrated in the information flow, too, when handling campaign response. The communication department that dialogs with the target groups about their needs via text, and basically any creative universe, needs to be working systematically with the given customer profiles. In addition, there's a data warehouse, which must be able to present and store relevant information about customers over time, as well as customer information that continuously must be adapted to a mix of customer behavior and company strategy. Even though we often look at our organization through an organization chart, where some people work in marketing and others in procurement and production, it does make more sense to see the organization as a large number of processes. These are processes that, across the different departments, create value chains to satisfy the organization's customers and their needs.

One example of a traditional value chain could be procurement of raw material, manufacturing, sales, delivery, and follow-up services. The mere fact that someone is part of this value chain means that he or she is measured at some point. We may not be calling it business analytics, but instead performance targets, budgets, or KPIs. Regardless of name, these are measuring instruments established to inform management functions about whether the established processes are achieving the organization's various targets.

Business analytics is relevant in both large and small businesses. As shown in the BA model in Chapter 1, it doesn't say anywhere that a company must be a large financial institution with thousands of data warehouse tables placed on large and expensive mainframes to deploy BA. Small and medium companies are known to carry out excellent BA in the most popular BA tool in the world: spreadsheets (as do large companies).

We have endeavored to make this technically complex discipline more easily accessible and digestible to a broader group of readers. Students at business schools with a couple of years' work experience should therefore be able to obtain maximum benefit from the book, too.

ORGANIZATION OF CHAPTERS

The book is structured in a way that shows the role of BA in the individual parts of this process and explains the relationship between these parts. You may read the chapters out of order, depending on the area that is of particular relevance to you. The intention of the book is to describe BA coherently and comprehensively while at the same time offering each chapter as a work of reference.

Compared to other publications on the subject, this book is less about describing the individual small subelements of BA, but more about demonstrating the link between them. Specific examples are offered showing how to add value in the business by using BA solutions.

In Chapter 1, we examine the BA model. The chapter covers the spectrum from business strategies to sourcing of data from the operational systems (data sources) as well as a case study. The model is the pivot of the subsequent Chapters 2 through 6, and the radio station case study illustrates a BA process, which will work as a point of reference throughout the subsequent chapters.

In Chapters 2 through 6, we go through the five layers of the BA model, each of which is allocated a chapter. Chapter 2 addresses the relationship between business strategies and the BA function. Chapter 3 focuses on the creation and use of information at a functional level. The question is how BA can work to support the improvement and maintenance of the company's various business processes (e.g., in sales, marketing, finance, management, and HR) so that they support the overall strategic goals as discussed in Chapter 2.

In Chapter 4, we look at business analytics through processes and present options as well as analytical methods for the transformation of data into information and knowledge.

In Chapter 5, we explain the functionality of a data warehouse and the processes in connection with the availability of data for business use.

In Chapter 6, we discuss the different operational systems and data sources in the organization's environment.

Chapter 7 shifts gears and focuses on the structuring of BA initiatives in so-called business intelligence competency centers (BICCs). Chapter 8 looks at how businesses can assess and prioritize BA projects and Chapter 9 focuses on the future of BA. The big question is "Where is business analytics heading?"

WHY THE TERM *BUSINESS ANALYTICS*?

This book could also have been given the title, "How to Make an Information Strategy," or "How to Use Information as a Strategic Asset," or simply "Business Intelligence." We chose the title *Business Analytics for Managers: Taking Business Intelligence beyond Reporting* because we felt that this is the next stepping-stone for companies in the information age of today. Today most business processes are linked together via electronic systems that allow them to run smoothly and in a coordinated way. The very same information systems generate electronic traces that we systematically collect and store all primarily for simple reporting purposes.

Business analytics allows business to go beyond traditional BA reporting. Had we therefore called our book "Business Intelligence," we feared that it would be bundled with all the technical literature on the subject that it attempts to counterbalance. We are entering the analytical age, a window in time where competitive advantages will be gained from companies making increasingly more advanced use of information. It will also be a period when other companies will fail and falter as *infosaurs*, with only muscles and armor and not the brainpower needed to survive in changing market conditions.

So to make it clear: *Analytics is an advanced discipline within business intelligence.* However, *business intelligence* as a term is today heavily associated with large software vendors that offer only simple technical reporting solutions for the end users. We will use the term *business analytics* in order to put extra focus on this missing element of the business intelligence equation, and which is by now the most exciting one. If mastered, this element will be what drives your company into a prosperous future.

CHAPTER 1

The Business Analytics Model

T he most important thing in a large and complex project with a large number of people and competencies involved is to create an overview of the project from a helicopter perspective as quickly as possible.

This chapter focuses on the business analytics (BA) model, which will help you get that overview. The model provides an outline for understanding—and creating—successful business analytics in any type of organization. The purpose of the model is to give the organization a single common frame of reference for an overall structure in the creation of successful BA, and it clarifies the roles of the individual contributors and the interaction in the information generation and information consumption process, which is what BA is, too. The model is the pivot of the rest of the book, and the five layers of the model are subsequently explained in detail with each layer allocated a separate chapter.

If your job is to make an information strategy, for example, as a CIO, the model comprises all the stakeholders and processes you should focus on. The model also gives clues about why most BA projects fail, which is simply because it is a large cross-organizational activity. You can compare it to a chain that is only as strong as its weakest link and if one of the departments involved is incompetent or if the knowledge handover between departments fails, your project will fail.

1

OVERVIEW OF THE BUSINESS ANALYTICS MODEL

The BA model in Exhibt 1.1 illustrates how business analytics is a layered and hierarchical discipline. Arrows show the underlying layers that are subject to layers above. Information requirements move from the business-driven environment down to the technically oriented environment. The subsequent information flow moves upward from the technically oriented environment toward the business-driven environment.

As illustrated by the BA model in Exhibit 1.1, there are many competencies, people, and processes involved in the creation of BA. In the top layer of the model, in the business-driven environment, the management specifies or develops an information strategy based on the company's or the business area's overall business strategy. In the second layer, the operational decision makers' need for information and knowledge is determined in a way that supports the

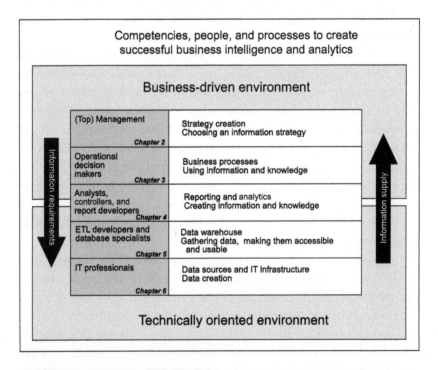

EXHIBIT 1.1 The Business Analytics Model

company's chosen strategy. In the middle layer of the model, analysts, controllers, and report developers create the information and knowledge to be used by the company's operational decision makers with the purpose of innovating and optimizing their day-to-day activities. In the second layer from the bottom, in the technically oriented environment in the data warehouse, the database specialist or the ETL (extract, transformation, load) developer merges and enriches data, and makes it accessible to the business user. In the bottom layer, in the technically oriented environment, the business's primary data generating source systems are run and developed by IT professionals from IT operations and development. Successful BA processes should have a fixed structure, which always begins with the specification of the information strategy, which is derived from the objectives of the business strategy.

Strategy Creation

All underlying contributions and activities must submit to the chosen information strategy, as specified in the business-driven environment at the top. The information strategy is decided at this level based on the organization's or the business area's overall business strategy (vision, mission, and objectives). Normally, these strategies will result in a number of key performance indicators (KPIs) with the purpose of measuring the degree of progress and success. The contents of the KPIs will depend on which underlying business process we want to control. The KPIs could, for instance, relate to profitability, return on equity (ROE), or different types of sales targets. The information strategy is often specified by the top management of the organization, by functional managers or business process owners. Large organizations may have an actual business development function, which is responsible for the formulation of the strategy for the entire group. How this is undertaken will be explained in detail in Chapter 2.

Business Processes and Information Use

Once the strategy, along with the overall strategic KPIs, is in place, a framework, focus, and objectives are established for the operational business processes and initiatives. The information and analyses shown in the underlying layers of the model must be directed at changing and managing business processes toward the strategic objectives made visible by the KPIs. The operational decision makers' desired behavior and the subsequent information and knowledge requirements to bring about this behavior are specified and outlined in this layer.

As mentioned, the objective of BA initiatives is to change business processes and actions so that they are targeted toward achieving the organization's strategic objectives. For example, operational decision makers from sales, marketing, production, general management, HR, and finance can use information and knowledge to optimize their daily activities. In Chapter 3, we'll look at what this means specifically for the various functions of the company.

Types of Reporting and Analytical Processes

In the analysis and reporting development environment in the middle of the model, analysts specify which information and data are necessary to achieve the desired behavior of operational managers in the business environment. This is where information and knowledge are generated about the deployment of analytical and statistical models, which are used on data from the data warehouse. The requirements for front-end applications, reporting, and functionality are also specified in detail here, all with the purpose of meeting the demands from the higher layers and levels of the model. Note that the analysis and reporting development environment is placed in the bordering area between the business-driven and the technically oriented environment, and that the team in this area usually has competencies in both areas. Chapter 4 covers more about the methodical work in the analytical and reporting environment.

Data Warehouse

Database specialists and ETL developers receive requirements from the analytical environment about data deliveries. If the required data is already in the warehouse, the process will be to make this data accessible to the front-end applications of the business. If data is not stored, the data warehouse will need to retrieve data from one or more operational data sources in the organization's environment. Alternatively, data can be purchased from an external supplier, or the IT department may be asked to implement a new infrastructure with a view to create a new operational data source. Chapter 5 focuses on methods and systems for storing, merging, and delivering data.

Data Sources: IT Operations and Development

Information technology operations and development must meet the requirements from the data warehouse about the delivery of data from the primary operational data sources or the development of new data sources. The different primary data sources in a company's environment and the data created are covered in Chapter 6.

As previously noted, a large number of people, competencies, and processes are involved in the creation of BA. Large organizations sometimes have several hundred people on all levels involved at the same time. In smaller companies, controllers and analysts must have a wide range of competencies to be able to carry out BA initiatives on their own.

It is important to realize that if something goes wrong in one of the layers of the BA model, the investment in BA may well be lost. If the management, in the top layer of the model, does not define one overall strategy, operational decision makers will not have a goal to work toward. The analyst won't know which analyses are required. It makes a big difference, for example, for the analyst to know whether the overall target is for the business to show a profit of $1.3 million after taxes, or whether the target is to be perceived as the most innovative enterprise—the two different targets require a completely different analytical approach and information deliverables. In data warehousing, the database specialist and the ETL developer won't know which data sources to retrieve, merge, enrich, and deliver to data marts (data prepared in the data warehouse for business use). Information technology operations and development won't be able to contribute by creating new data sources, since they don't know which new information and knowledge is required by the business. In other words, the whole thing becomes a messy affair without focus. One way of avoiding such a chaotic situation is to create a business intelligence competency center (BICC), perhaps as a virtual organizational unit. We'll take a closer look at BICC in Chapter 7.

DEPLOYMENT OF THE BA MODEL

> *Of course, this is what we've always been doing or tried to do—but it's the first time I am able to put it into words and see our endeavors in a useful analytical model.*
> —Program manager for a large radio station

Case Study: How to Make an Information Strategy for a Radio Station

Now that we've introduced our theoretical model, let's apply this information to a concrete example in order to understand it better. This case study features the BA initiative of a large radio station that broadcasts nationwide. The case study is a simplified and somewhat creative version of real events, and its objective is merely to outline a BA process. Focus is on the helicopter perspective, an improved conceptual tool, and the first important insights. The case study relates to the BA model in Exhibit 1.1.

Overall Strategic Targets of the Business

The radio station's vision is that there is a demand for radio entertainment in the shape of good music, entertaining talk, and news. Its mission is to become a leading player in the national market. The station's specified business goal is a market share of 25% and a return on equity (ROE) of 15%. The executive management cockpit or dashboard of the radio station with KPIs for monitoring business performance in relation to strategic objectives is illustrated in Exhibit 1.2.

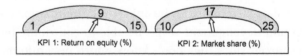

KPI 1: Return on equity (%)	KPI 2: Market share (%)

EXHIBIT 1.2 Executive Management Cockpit of Radio Station with KPIs Prior to BA Initiative

The current status, which can be read from the instruments in the executive management cockpit, is an actual ROE of 9% and an actual market share of 17%. So the station has a way to go in order to achieve its targets of an ROE of 15% and a market share of 25%. The business strategy and objectives are thus presented by means of the following metrics (measures) or KPIs. Note that success and good performance are derived from the actual values of these measures in relation to the objectives.

Goal(KPI 1): ROE = 15%. Actual = 9%

Goal (KPI 2): Market share = 25%. Actual 17%

The two KPIs are used to control and manage the radio station. Return on equity (KPI 1) is the most important KPI, and it is affected by the market share (KPI 2). The thinking is that a bigger market share (KPI 2) will mean more concurrent listeners and increased advertising revenue, which means a bigger ROE for a given level of cost. A new BA initiative is planned and implemented in the business. The process is outlined in the following section using the BA model.

Functional Strategy and Business Case

Business analytics activities must always be based on the business-driven environment, with the management specifying or creating one single information strategy, which must be subject to the company's overall business strategy (vision, mission, and objectives).

The Program Manager has come up with a strategic initiative to increase the business's market share from the current 17% to 25%. The radio station must hold on to its listeners longer. The Program Manager specifies this strategy as: "From our current record of holding on to our listeners for 15 minutes, before he or she changes channel, we must in the future hold on to our average listener for 30 minutes." The Program Manager introduces the performance target: average listening time as a new measure or KPI for the production department and the target is that the average listener must be kept on the broadcasting frequency for 30 minutes. The average listening time thus takes its place as a new KPI on the management dashboard.

Target for KPI 3: Average listening time = 30 minutes.

Actual = 15 minutes

Note that this strategic target penetrates right into the core business of the radio station. If the target—to hold on to the average listener for 30 minutes—is achieved, it will mean a bigger market share, increased advertising revenue, and, ultimately, an improved ROE. So, it is expected that an increase in KPI 3 will affect both KPI 2 and KPI 1 positively.

Before launching the BA initiative, the Program Manager prepares a business case for the project. He expects a larger market share (KPI 2) of up to 25%, as a result of the increase in average listening time (KPI 3) of 30 minutes. This is expected to improve the pricing of advertising slots, so that the advertising revenues of the radio station increase by $4 million per year. Based on these expectations, he calculates that return on equity (KPI 1) will increase from 9% to 13%. In addition, he expects that the BA initiative will incur a resource consumption of three employees in four months as well as necessitate purchasing software and consultancy services for $250,000.

Total costs are estimated to be $1 million. The business case speaks in favor of carrying out the project. The reason is an expected growth in the annual cash flow of $4 million from increased advertising revenue, and that the project will cost only $1 million to implement.

Moreover, the payback period is only one quarter and the project is not considered to entail any risk. Note that if the business case had shown a negative result (or if the project had looked risky), the BA initiative should not be implemented. Business cases are a good way of evaluating and prioritizing BA projects. We'll cover more about business cases in Chapter 8.

The management of the radio station now has the first elements of its information strategy in place, and it's directly related to the overall strategic objectives of the business.

Business Processes and Actions

The business processes of the production department must now be adjusted in such a way that they actively show a behavior that secures the average listener for longer, thereby increasing the value of KPI 3.

There is an acknowledgment among the staff that they need more information and knowledge about their listeners' characteristics and preferences at different times and in connection with the different programs. In other words, the processes must be adapted to a listener profile, to enable the DJs and newsreaders of the radio station to continuously deliver content that is to the current listeners' tastes. In the future, the radio production must be based on factual knowledge about the current listeners' characteristics and preferences. This means that whatever is broadcasted must be customized to suit current listeners' interests, and results must be measurable on an ongoing basis and readable on the management dashboard—now with the three measures or KPIs: KPI 1: return on equity, KPI 2: market share, and KPI 3: average listening time.

Analytical Processes and Front-ends

In the analytical environment, it is the task of the analyst to create information and knowledge to drive business processes in the direction of delivering content that, to a greater extent, falls into the listeners' tastes. The main questions for the analyst are:

- Who are our listeners?
- What do they like to listen to?
- Who listens to what and when?

The analyst quickly realizes that he does not possess sufficient data about the listeners to be able to work out listener profiles. If he did have this data, it could be merged with the program database of the radio station in the data warehouse, and subsequently constitute the basis of the creation of knowledge about listener profiles at different times and for the different programs of the radio station.

Data Warehouse

The analyst needs the data warehouse to provide him with data on the listeners' ages, genders, and tastes and preferences 24/7. He needs this information for the profiles. The database specialist does not have this data stored, and it cannot be obtained from an external supplier. Therefore, the database specialist asks the IT department to create a new operational data source to collect data on listener profiles at different times of the day.

Data Sources: IT Operations and Development

Information technology operations and development decide to collect data on the listeners' ages, genders, tastes, moods, and listening times via a questionnaire. They develop an electronic questionnaire that listeners can complete on the radio station's Web site. The survey is announced and promoted on air, and sponsor prizes are given out via a prize drawing for the participating listeners. The data-collection process enables the creation of new operational data sources in the technically oriented environment, and the process is controlled and managed by developers and operational staff from IT operations and development. Using ETL tools, the database specialist or the ETL developer now continuously transfers the new data source into the data warehouse. Here it is merged with the other databases of the radio station (for instance, the database on past aired radio programs). After having been merged, the data is moved out into a data mart area so that the analyst can access them.

In the analytical environment, the analyst now has access to data and starts to transform the collected and merged data from the data warehouse into information and knowledge. The result of his analytical processes using statistical methods and tools such as data mining shows that the typical listener in the early hours of the morning is a fun-loving 30-year-old woman.

The analyst also has report-developing competencies and has prepared a front-end report with the results from his BA tool, which could be Microsoft Excel. The report contains information and knowledge about listener profiles for different times of the day and for the different programs. The report is released weekly with new numbers to the business's intranet, where it can be accessed and used by business users in the production department. Note that the analytical environment is positioned in the border area between the technically oriented environment and the business-driven environment, and we find people with competencies in both areas. The front-end solution and the report could also be delivered by a report developer from the technically oriented environment, based on results from the analytical processes.

The radio station's operational decision makers, DJs, and newsreaders must now change their daily business processes and actions in such a way that their actions provide better support for the achievement of the strategic targets of the business. As mentioned, the strategic target for the production department is to hold on to listeners for longer with a view to increase market share and ultimately improve return on equity. In the morning, they all read the released front-end report to make use of the information and knowledge from the controller's analytical processes. Before each DJ puts on a song, he looks at the BA report and asks himself the question: Is a fun-loving 30-year-old woman going to like this music?

If he's about to play a heavy metal CD, it'll probably go back on the shelf. Instead, "Material Girl" by Madonna stands a good chance. Equally, all news will be sorted through by the newsreader. Before reading any news, he now asks himself the question: Is a fun-loving 30-year-old woman going to find this piece of news interesting?

If the news is about motoring, it'll probably end up in the paper bin, whereas news about either the current economic crises or the latest cinema film is likely to be broadcasted.

What is happening on this radio station is business analytics. Decision support delivered to operational decision makers based on data analysis (creation of knowledge). The purpose of the exercise is to direct the decision makers' daily business processes toward achieving strategic targets.

Evaluation of the BA Process

Over the next six months, the radio station succeeds in holding on to its average listener for 9 minutes longer than before and all three KPIs are improved. (See Exhibit 1.3.)

EXHIBIT 1.3 The Radio Station's Dashboard with KPIs after BA Initiative

Following the BA initiative, the radio station's average listener stayed tuned in for an average of 24 minutes (KPI 3). The radio station's market share (KPI 2) went up to 20%, and return on equity (KPI 1) increased to 12%. The business is on its way to achieving its overall strategic targets, and the production department's BA initiative must be said to have been successful. It could not have been done without BA—from strategy to data sources.

CONCLUSIONS

The purpose of the case study was, as mentioned, to provide a quick overview and to show how BA can be deployed successfully to support and influence the behavior of operational decision makers with a view to achieving overall business targets.

The 12 most important conclusions to draw from the case study in terms of the establishment of successful BA are:

- The BA initiative of a business area or a department must support and promote the department's overall strategic targets, which equally must support and promote the overall strategic targets of the business as a whole. We will take a closer look at the relationship between business strategies and the BA function in Chapter 2.

- The strategic targets of the BA activities of a given business area must be measurable with one or more KPIs to ensure that performance and progress can be followed on an ongoing basis. The chosen KPI, or KPIs, must be able to influence the overall KPIs of the company. More about KPIs in Chapter 3.

- A planned BA activity must stand up to an evaluation based on business case principles. In other words, a BA initiative must create value for the company just like any other investment. Increased revenue or savings must justify the investment. More about business cases and the prioritization of BA projects in Chapter 8.

- It must be specified what kind of information and knowledge are required for the operational decision makers, and how they are to act on this information. This part needs to be taken very seriously. It's important to understand that it is here and only here, in the process-changing area, that BA creates value for the company. In all other contexts, BA is just a cost. More about this subject in Chapter 3.

■ The analyst/controller must be able to decode business users correctly, and specify the requirement for relevant data and use the right methods, so that useful information and knowledge are presented for decision support. Front-end applications and reports conveying knowledge must have correct functionality and be simple and intuitive for business users. More about analyses and reporting methods in Chapter 4.

■ The data specialist or the ETL developer in the data warehouse must be able to merge and enrich data with useful dimensions and perspectives. Data quality must be very high to ensure credibility from the business side. More about data warehouse and data quality in Chapter 5.

■ Information technology operations and development must be able to establish an infrastructure for new data sources and secure valid retrieval of source data. More about data sources in Chapter 6.

■ The achievement of BA in large organizations is a process that involves contributions from many functions and people. The BA model provides a helpful overview of structure, people, and activities. So it's necessary to use it in the planning stages of BA initiatives. It may help to create an organizational function to handle BA activities across the functions of the organization to ensure the necessary coordination. More about the organization of BA in Chapter 7.

■ The analyst/controller will typically be a key person in BA activities and represent a kind of cross-functional person holding all the strings together. This is because of his or her presence in both the business-driven environment and the technically oriented environment (refer back to the BA model). The analyst will usually have the necessary insight into processes and strategies in the business-driven environment as well as the necessary technical insight to be able to enter into a constructive dialogue with the data warehouse and IT department.

▪ Business analytics is a holistic and hierarchical discipline, stretching from business strategies to sourcing from operational data sources. The business-driven environment must assume full ownership and manage the process. The technically oriented environment must support the process with infrastructure, data delivery, and the necessary application functionality.

▪ Business analytics is a support process. It can be seen as a chain that is only as strong as its weakest link. If, for instance, the analyst cannot derive the right information from data, then all other activities are of no use. The same is true if we do not deliver the right data to the analysts, or if the business users chooses not to act based on the new knowledge. In Chapter 8, we take a closer look at what to be aware of as project manager of a BA project.

▪ Successful BA processes should have a fixed structure, which always begins with the specification of the information strategy, which is derived from the objectives of the business strategy. Sketching an information strategy of the radio station using the BA model is visualized in Exhibit 1.4.

EXHIBIT 1.4   Sketching an Information Strategy

Who	What to Do	Radio Station Example
Executive management function CEOs	Executive management sets overall strategic targets for the business.	Executive management sets overall business targets: Return on equity (KPI 1) = 15% Market share (KPI 2) = 25%
Business function Functional managers/ directors and operational decision makers in HR, sales, production, marketing, finance, etc.	Functional managers/ directors set strategic target at the functional level.	Program Manager sets target; Average listening time (KPI 3) = 30 minutes
	Operational decision makers improve upon business processes using information created by the BA function.	DJs and newsreaders improve their processes by broadcasting music and news in accordance with listeners' tastes at different times of the day.
	Operational decision makers demand and use information.	DJs and newsreaders demand information about listeners' tastes/profiles at different times of the day
BA function Analyst, controller, data manager, and report developer	Identify business requirements and create information using analytical methodology.	Analyst identifies listeners' profiles at different times of the day by using data mining methodology, and report developer creates reports.
Data warehouse function ETL developer and database specialist	Gather, enrich, and supply data for business use, based on requirements from analyst.	ETL developer and database specialist gather, enrich, store and deliver data on the listeners' age, gender, tastes, moods, and listening times, based on requirements from analyst.
Data source and IT infrastructure function IT professionals	Maintain and develop IT infrastructure for data to be created.	IT professional creates new source data by developing an electronic questionnaire on the Web site to be completed by radio station listeners, based on requirements from the data warehouse team.

CHAPTER 2

Business Analytics at the Strategic Level

This is the first of five chapters that describe the business analytics (BA) model. The chapter focuses on the strategic level and is primarily written for those who deliver or request information in connection with the development of business strategies.

We present a number of scenarios that have a varying degree of coordination between the development of strategies in a company and the role of BA. While reading the scenarios, reflect on where your organization is based on these perspectives. Similarly, consider where in this context your strategies fit. It also makes sense to consider whether the organization has understood and achieved the full potential inherent in BA and, if not, whether more effort should be put into driving the deployment of BA. Other angles from which to read this chapter are: Where are my competitors today? What kind of market will we be operating in five years from now? And, if the market is significantly changed compared to today, do we intend to lead or follow the competition on the information front?

The focus of this chapter is therefore not on how to develop a business strategy; many other books describe this very well. Instead, our aim is to demonstrate important relationships between overall business strategies and the information that the BA function can deliver in this context. Behind all the discussions, there are always the two key questions: How can the BA function influence the overall strategy process in the organization? How does the overall business strategy subsequently influence the BA function?

LINK BETWEEN STRATEGY AND THE DEPLOYMENT OF BA

To facilitate our discussion of various degrees of integration between strategy and BA functions, we'll offer an outline of the concept of strategy and how it is created. A *strategy* is a description of the overall way in which a business is run. It typically covers a year at a time. Its purpose is to adapt the organization's business area, resources, and activities to the market in which the organization operates. As a rule of thumb, a strategy attempts to handle company issues in the short run while at the same time trying to create competitive advantages in the long run. To be concrete, strategy is developed by defining a number of specific and measurable targets to be achieved by individual parts of the organization. The specified targets are often supported by some expectations—which can be more or less precise—as to how the individual department should achieve these targets.

The strategy process usually runs once a year, and will often contain a substantial element of adaptation of last year's strategy in relation to new circumstances and expectations for next year. Of course, this will vary between different types of businesses and markets. Sometimes an organization will develop a strategy from scratch, but this usually happens only as part of a complete change of leadership, or if an organization decides that the old strategy has failed or is no longer viable. A strategy development process is a mixture of analyses, each of which is based on different data sources or methods or both. Our focus is business analytics, and we will therefore focus on the delivery of information based on data from a data warehouse.

In a strategic or overall management context, information is used to change and coordinate business procedures in the other functional areas of the organization. The reason for our use of the word *coordinate* is that strategic management should not be seen as a number of *serial* actions, but rather as a number of *parallel* actions, in a number of departments, that must be coordinated.

It is sometimes said that strategy is like bringing up children—it is not essential that you always do the right thing, but it is essential that you are consistent. This means that it is essential to coordinate the activities in the organization so that they are all moving in the same direction. A strategy development process has a purpose: to update a number of elements such as the company's vision, which is about long-term goals, and to update its mission, which is a brief outline of how management intends to achieve these goals. A strategy should represent not only the general plans for how to act in the next few years but also some targets that, specifically and expressed in numbers, describe the results of the strategy over the next period of time.

STRATEGY AND BA: FOUR SCENARIOS

In the following sections, we present four scenarios that illustrate different degrees of integration between the BA function and the company's strategy. The purpose of these scenarios is to prompt the reader to consider where his or her organization is in relation to these scenarios. The scenarios can also give some insights into whether the organization has understood and achieved the full potential inherent in BA, and thus whether more effort should go into optimizing and maturing the deployment of BA.

Exhibit 2.1 shows an outline of the four scenarios. The way we describe the link between strategy and BA will also constitute the basis of the rest of this chapter.

Scenario 1 is "no formal link between strategy and BA." Companies that are separated in their strategy, without data or with limited data distributed over a large number of source systems, are typically unable to make a link between corporate strategy and BA. In these companies, data is not used for decision making at a strategic level. Instead, data is used in connection with ad hoc retrieval for the answering of concrete questions along the way, but without any link to business strategy. Many companies have realized that they do not have the data, the staff, or the technology to perform the task. Seen from a strategic perspective, a maturing process could be initiated.

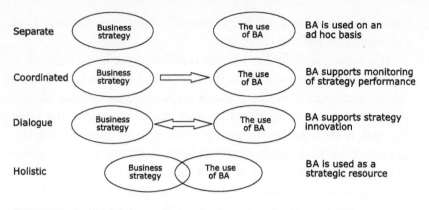

EXHIBIT 2.1 Link between Strategy and BA

Alternatively, the company just continues with a business strategy that is not based on information.

Scenario 2 is "BA supports strategy at a functional level." If companies, in connection with the implementation of a strategy, request that the BA function perform monitoring of individual functions' achievement of targets, we have coordination between strategy and BA. However, if there is no flow back from BA to the strategic level, then the BA function is reactive in relation to the strategy function. In this case, the role of BA is merely to produce reports supporting the performance of individual departments.

Scenario 3 is "dialogue between the strategy and the BA functions." If the organization makes sure that individual functions optimize its behavior based on BA information, but that the strategy function, too, takes part in the learning loop, we'll get a BA function that proactively supports the strategy function. A learning loop is facilitated when the BA function is reporting on business targets *and* is providing analyses as well as differences between targets and actuals, with the objective of improving both future strategies and the individual departments' performance.

Scenario 4 is "information as a strategic resource." The characteristic of the fourth scenario is that information is being treated as a strategic resource, which can be used to determine strategy. Companies that fit this scenario will systematically while analyzing the opportunities and threats of the market think how information, in combination with their strategies, can give them a competitive advantage.

The four phases represent a maturity, ability, and willingness to work with information on different levels. We can't really say that one level is better than another. The appropriate level must be chosen based on a strategic perspective. In some industries, BA information is not essential to business success, while in others it will be a central competitive parameter. Sometimes, as in Scenario 1, it's a simple matter of realizing that the company does not possess the data, the staff, or the technology to perform the task. Seen from a strategic perspective, the option exists to take steps toward the next phase, or to choose an alternative business strategy that is less information dependent.

Scenario 1: No Formal Link between Strategy and BA

The first type of link between the deployment of BA and strategy is the absence of any link. It is in itself a surprising notion that this can be the case. But the most common explanation is that, when developing their strategy, companies often focus on the most visible aspects, such as sales targets, production targets, or cost targets in connection with procurement. In relation with the achievement of these targets, the sales department, production, and procurement will be faced with targets based on the business strategy. However, a company consists of many other functions such as HR, finance, product development, strategy, competitive analysis, administration, and BA. These functions are called *support functions* because they are not adding value in connection with the daily production. However, if they did not exist, the company would encounter problems in the long run.

From a strategic perspective the supporting functions are of course expected to support the primary and value creating processes. This may happen when the support functions themselves interpret the business strategy in their daily activities, but more often by the owners of the primary processes placing demands on services from the support functions based on their targets. So when we describe a scenario with no link between strategy and BA, it is not a question of completely un-coordinated entities, but rather a case of a filter existing between them. A filter may exist because it is primarily the individual processes owners on an ad hoc basis and not the strategy that defines which information is to be generated by the BA function.

The consequence of the filter is that the BA function prioritizes its tasks according to what best serves the daily target achievement of the company instead of what is best for long-term strategic projects. Moreover, the BA function tasks are performed based on the driving force of different users requesting information. In terms of reporting, this will result in the development of more or less authorized reports with inconsistent presentations of the business that they are describing. All in all, the quality of BA in this type of organization will typically be an assessment of how quickly a question is answered and how well-founded the answer is.

Other reasons why there is no formalized link between the strategy and the BA functions may be that the right conditions simply do not exist. There are situations, such as small businesses with one or few customers, where the cost of running a data warehouse is bigger than the value of the decision support created. And there are companies that define their strategic targets in a way that is not measurable. If, for instance, a company defines a target to be "we need to establish better relations with our suppliers," then that may be difficult to quantify. Because this definition does not tell us what to measure, we must ask: Is it the number of complaints, average time per transaction, or the quality of their deliveries that are to be improved via this new strategy?

Scenario 2: BA Supports Strategy at a Functional Level

The second scenario represents what we call an *adapted information strategy*. Here the BA function is a reactive element, solely employed in connection with the monitoring of whether the defined targets of the strategy are achieved. We have illustrated this process in Exhibit 2.2. The recipients of these reports or key performance indicators (KPIs) are the individual departments, which means that there is no feedback to the strategic level. The BA function supports company performance proactively, but only reactively in terms of company strategy. There may be a formalized dialogue between individual functions and BA, but the relation to the strategy function is formalized as a monologue, from strategy to BA function.

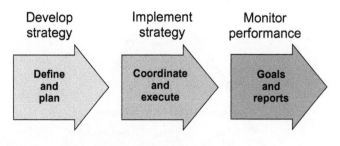

EXHIBIT 2.2 BA Supports Performance

In terms of the quality of BA in such an organization, it's important to be good at defining targets based on strategy. These are targets that relate to each other internally and that, combined, make up a whole. It is equally important that the BA function is technically competent when it comes to operationalizing these targets via reports and making those reports both accessible to users and also full of the most updated information possible.

Based on a strategy development process, individual departments define a number of specific requirements, or targets, they are to achieve. Sometimes a target will simply be given to the sales department: It must increase revenue by 10% over the previous year. Alternatively, the department may be given additional information about which segments to grow and with which products. There may also be a message that this must be brought about in cooperation with other departments, such as marketing. Based on the given targets, it will then be up to the individual functions—with various degrees of autonomy—to decide how they are going to achieve these targets.

We have illustrated this process in Exhibit 2.3, where a substrategy for HR is developed. In this case, the requirement from the company's overall strategy could be to reduce absence due to illness by 10%. How to achieve this will not necessarily be specified. Consequently, the HR department itself will have to come up with an HR strategy that specifies how it intends to meet the target and a deadline for its achievement given by the company's strategy. In the same way, a substrategy needs to be developed for customer relationship management (CRM), the CRM strategy, and a substrategy for the production department, the production strategy.

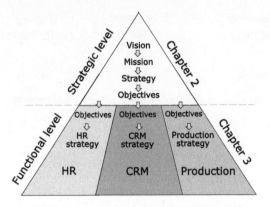

EXHIBIT 2.3   The Relationships between Strategic Level and Functional Level

Five Requirements for Targets

It is important to determine what information may be relevant to the company when developing its strategy and when monitoring whether this strategy is being achieved. In connection with the monitoring of the strategy, a number of targets to be achieved are outlined. These targets may be few and general, and it will then be up to the individual departments to define who will be doing what. In other cases, the targets will be specified in great detail and the departments will have little room for maneuvering. It applies to all targets, however, that there are some formal requirements that they must meet. These are basic requirements to ensure that measurements can be operationalized. For when is it that we must expect to see the increase in the number of our customers by 20%? How do we define our customers? If, halfway through the year, we see an increase of our customer base of only 8%, is that then a problem or to be expected? We also need to ensure that if we find targets that look as if they will not be achieved, we can actually pinpoint the person responsible, who can then react to this information. Five updated target requirements follow. Some of the requirements are necessary for the technical establishment of benchmarks; others are concerned with who must take action if the benchmarks deviate in a critical way from the specified targets. The requirements we make to benchmarks are that they must be:

- **Specific:** Targets, such as how many customers we must have by the end of the year, what our revenue must be, by how much we must reduce delivery times, and so forth.

- **Measurable:** If it's not measurable, it's not a relevant target. If we do not know how many customers we have, we need to find another target. If it's not possible to allocate revenue and costs to the processes we want to improve, we need to establish some other targets.

- **Agreed:** The organization must accept the targets. If this is not the case, there is no ownership and the organization is about to implement a strategy that, at best, will be ignored or, at worst, will be counteracted. It is implicit, too, that accepted targets mean that we have some specific individuals who are directly responsible for the given targets.

- **Realistic:** Targets must be realistic. Often, targets are accepted without standing a chance of being achieved. This may have something to do with the corporate culture, maybe someone is trying to buy time, or that there are no consequences involved in not achieving the targets.

- **Time-bound:** What is the deadline for reducing costs to a certain level and raising customer loyalty up a level? It's also important that we are able, at an early stage, to determine that targets are not being achieved as expected in order that we can make corrections.

If you put the initial letters of the five words together, you get the acronym SMART. Note that the business literature might offer some variations in the meaning of the five words, but the underlying concepts are the same as those given here.

There are a number of business reasons as to why objectives need to be SMART. Seen in a BA context, objectives need to be specific, measurable, and time-bound so that they can be defined and operationalized in the first place. If they are not, we won't know, when implementing the technical solution, which information to collect and calculate so that it describes the overall objective of the desired process. If the objectives are not measurable, we cannot quantify them technically and thus measure them on an ongoing basis. Likewise, objectives need to be time-bound if an information system is to be able to deliver messages to users, when critical values are exceeded.

In a broader business context, the five requirements work to ensure a clear-cut understanding of the basis of business initiatives. If objectives are not specific, they may be interpreted differently, which leads to different versions of the truth. If objectives are not measurable, people will start debating whether customers are loyal enough. If you do not have ways of measuring something, you must create ways of measuring it—just like in the radio station case study in Chapter 1. For technical reasons, too, it's essential that benchmarks be time-specific, since the entire establishment of a data warehouse is about relating pieces of information and creating a historic view. If we are to deliver efficient reporting, the time dimension must be clearly defined. We prefer to automate the measuring via a data warehouse, so that users on a continuous basis can retrieve data about the achievement of targets. However, customer information, such as "brand awareness," will typically be distributed through reports. Consequently, we do not need to be able to retrieve all objectives from a data warehouse, but it's generally preferred, because it means that there will only ever be one version of the truth, and that this truth can be delivered whenever users so desire and in an aggregated form.

Scenario 3: Dialogue between the Strategy and the BA Functions

The third scenario is based on the existence of an established data warehouse to integrate and store data, as well as an established BA function with analytical competencies to make use of this data. We are typically looking at a significant investment in software and employees. This scenario is also characterized by a continuous dialogue between the strategy and the BA functions. The reporting methods used at this level for the managing and measuring of operational processes now begin to have different names such as business performance management (BPM) systems, scorecards, and customer profitability/segment analyses. This signifies that a flow of information is going back to the strategy function based on the created reports.

The information described in this section is feedback information from scorecards and BPM solutions. These types of solutions are normally cyclical and start with a strategy. Based on the strategy, three things occur: benchmarking is carried out; there is then an ongoing measuring and analyzing of deviation from targets; and finally, based on the analyses, the strategy is adapted and optimized. We will take a closer look at this in this chapter's section "Corporate Strategy's Subsequent Requirements to BA." Quality for the BA function in this scenario is the ability to deliver relevant information to the strategy function. This is done in order that the strategy may be adapted on an ongoing basis for the organization to accommodate changes in the market and within the organization itself. When reports are produced describing whether individual departments are meeting their KPIs, action will, of course, be taken if any major deviations between targets and the achievements are shown. There will therefore always be some form of feedback between target achievement and strategy, although this feedback process may be more or less formalized. An example of the conceptualization of the feedback processes is found in corporate performance management (CPM) and score carding. As Exhibit 2.4 illustrates, this is an ongoing cycle, where the enterprise as its starting point has defined a strategy to be implemented in the various departments that make up the business. Coordination is performed by identifying the so-called *critical success factors*, which are the elements that are essential to whether the strategy is successful, and making sure that they are coordinated. This is typically done via internal meetings across functions. It is at this stage, too, that we define who is responsible for the various KPIs, and thus who must react to these and in what way.

When the strategy is set in motion, progress is measured on an ongoing basis. Generally speaking, KPIs are rarely hit accurately, but rather a bit over or under. In both cases, learning can be derived based on analyses. Did we overlook any potential opportunities, or do we perhaps lack certain competencies in the organization? An optimization of the strategy takes place when we use this learning to improve our business processes and thereby ensure that the organization

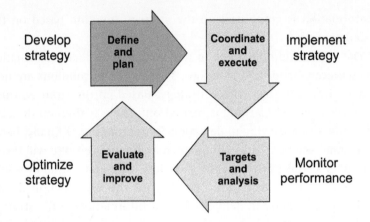

EXHIBIT 2.4 Feedback Processes and Learning at the Strategic Level

maintains its agility between the annual strategy processes. And experiences from previous strategy iterations can contribute to create learning in terms of the strategy for the coming iteration.

An alternative way of operationalizing strategic feedback processes is via the "balanced scorecard," a method introduced in the early 1990s. It connects corporate strategy with the internal processes that will be realizing them, connects it with customer loyalty and, finally—and this was the new thing—with the organization's internal competencies. What the balanced scorecard achieves, therefore, is to link the primary production processes to the development of the business. If we cannot produce enough, do we then employ more people or different people, or do we establish a dialogue with our employees and on that basis reward them differently? The method, which was developed by Kaplan and Norton, represents a cornerstone for how to formulate requirements in connection with the implementation of a new strategy.

Scenario 4: Information as a Strategic Resource

The fourth scenario is about information being regarded as a strategic resource. Such enterprises are characterized by using their analyses of market strengths and weaknesses by systematically thinking about how this information, combined with their strategies, can give them a competitive advantage. As illustrated by Exhibit 2.5, this is less about

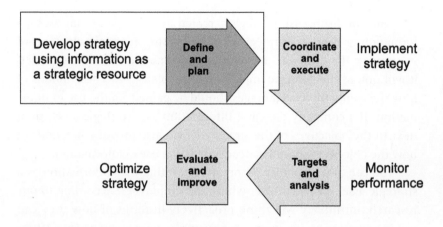

EXHIBIT 2.5 Information as a Strategic Resource

technical solutions and more about people competencies that are required in the strategy development process. In some cases, this may mean that the enterprise needs to ensure it has staff with both strategic and information knowledge represented at the top management level. This is not an altogether surprising conclusion, considering that we live in the age of information.

A typical example of an enterprise that focuses on information as a strategic resource is Amazon.com, which sells books via the Internet. Here information is saved about the individual customer's purchases and requests, and these are then processed, with the result that customers are subsequently greeted with offers that are relevant and of service to them. This is a case of improving the relevance of offers to customers based on information, which differentiates Amazon.com in a positive way from other Internet-based book shops. This trend is emerging among certain retail chains, too, where the segmentation of customers means that services can be customized to local conditions. Moreover, we see a growing sale of information from shops to the manufacturers of the goods sold in the shops. This information describes which types of people buy their products, how price-sensitive the products are, which products are typically sold together, and so forth. This feedback constitutes essential information for manufacturers in terms of product development, pricing, and promotion in the right places with the right messages.

You can distinguish strategies created by a company that uses information or data as a strategic asset by looking at certain elements of its strategy. If a company does not use information as a strategic asset, it will not, in the strategic implementation plans, have descriptions of how the competitive advantages should be gained via the use of information. If a company does use information as a strategic asset, then next to the objectives of the strategy it will also provide directions of how the objectives should be reached via the use of information.

You can also recognize an organization that uses information as a strategic asset on its culture, where the employees, according to our research, intuitively will think proactively in terms of how they can use information to overcome, for example, a new competitive situation. This sort of a culture will use the information as a strategic asset as a result of a top-down process as well as a bottom-up process. This means that if one region learns to improve its processes via the use of information, the news will be captured by the strategy team, and spread as a best practice to the rest of the organization as a result of the next strategy creation process.

In Chapter 3, which focuses on business analytics at the functional level, we present a case in which the strategy at the functional level is largely managed on the basis of data warehouse information. Quality in this context is, therefore, being able to understand how the use of information can provide enterprises with an advantage in terms of key competitive parameters. Information at a strategic level must therefore be understood centrally in connection with the strategy development process and throughout the organization where the implementation is carried out. Nonprofit organizations need to consider *how* information is used and regard it as a central leverage in terms of the performance of tasks, which are defined in the organization's objectives and strategy. As previously discussed, the use of information as a strategic resource is first about identifying central competitive parameters, and second about understanding how this information can ensure that the enterprise differentiates itself from its competitors. We have chosen to introduce a tool that will help you determine which information is going to support your organization's business-critical initiatives, as well as provide you with a number of examples of how this works in specific terms.

WHICH INFORMATION DO WE PRIORITIZE?

The BA function needs to deliver information to the strategy development process. Naturally, it's not always possible to know exactly and at all times which information to deliver. However, based on an analysis of which competitive parameters an enterprise experiences in the market, we can tell which type of information to focus on. That is not to say that any information can be ruled out as irrelevant in advance, but in a world of constant decisions on focus and the prioritization of tasks due to limited resources, some information will have an obvious priority.

We have been inspired by Treacy and Wiersema's article from 1993, "Three Paths to Market Leadership." Treacy and Wiersema describe how any enterprise, in principle, can become a market leader if it masters one of the following three disciplines and matches its competition on the two others.

The first discipline is about being strong in the field of product innovation and being a leading supplier of "state of the art" products. One example of this could be when Sony first launched its Walkman or, at the time of writing, its Blu-ray technology. The second discipline is about having strong customer relations, that is, about being able to establish a psychological connection to customers. Apple seems to have this ability, which causes some buyers to have a near-religious relationship with the brand. Another example is Telecom Enterprises, with their customer loyalty programs which attempts to strengthen the relationship between the individual customer and a commercial organization. Finally, we have the operational excellence discipline, which is about being efficient in relation to production and delivery services, and which always focuses on optimizing internal processes. In Exhibit 2.6, the enterprise has no clear focus on any of the three value disciplines, though with some preference to the Customer Intimacy approach to the market.

In the real world, however, businesses do not just compete on one of these parameters, but on a combination of all three. Therefore, when analyzing one's business, it's a good exercise to consider how much focus is given to each of the three strategies, and thus receive an overview of which information structure best supports corporate strategies.

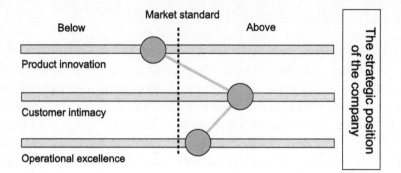

EXHIBIT 2.6 The Three Disciplines for Market Leadership

In Exhibit 2.6, we've included something called *market standard*. This obviously depends on how you define your market. Does iPhone belong to the consumer gadgets market or the telephone manufacturers market? The answer to such a question may be given via the business's mission, which defines the market and how the enterprise should be differentiated, but in the end it does come down to a subjective evaluation. Based on this, the business obtains an image of the competition and thereby some kind of market standard.

In the following section, we explain the three disciplines (perspectives) in more depth and we look at the information that the BA function needs to deliver to support these. In relation to the four scenarios, we are definitely in the third one, where the BA function delivers information to the strategy function. We might be in the fourth scenario as well, but this depends entirely on whether the people responsible for the development of strategies understand and uses the scope and potential of BA while developing future strategies.

The Product and Innovation Perspective

This perspective is highly prioritized by enterprises that act based on "product innovation" or "product leadership" strategies, that is, businesses that adopt as their central competitive parameter that their products and services can be characterized as "state-of-the-art." Focus is therefore typically on technological aspects and all the things their products are able to do. These are usually enterprises delivering technical sales to specialists. Examples include server solutions, data warehouse solutions, road paving, and windmills.

The knowledge these businesses normally use to differentiate themselves in the market is therefore closely linked to technological knowledge about product development and, to a lesser extent, to knowledge about customer behavior (customer intimacy strategy), or knowledge about how to efficiently produce and deliver services and products (operational excellence strategy). Note that we will be mentioning and discussing some statistical methods throughout the rest of this chapter, these statistical methods will all be presented in greater detail in Chapter 4. Moreover, keep in mind that the analyses presented in this book are primarily built on data warehouse information. One analysis that will always have priority is which products deliver the highest revenue, since this is key to the development of future strategies. In other words, you look at the sales price and deduct all direct costs related to manufacturing and distribution as well as the sales and marketing of the product. Development costs are not taken into consideration here, since attention is given to analyzing internal operational processes.

The purpose of this exercise is to shift focus from the number of sold units of different product types and onto the products that deliver profit. Moreover, the profit per product unit will be an important input for further analyses from the product and segment perspective.

In the market, analyses are prepared by enterprises on a continuous basis, and models are developed to describe the state of the current market, as well as how this market can be expected to change in the future. Combined with forecasting models for individual products, this can give some useful estimates of where revenue will be earned in the future. These analyses should be supported by the historical knowledge, too, which we stored from the life cycles of comparable products, information that can be expected to be delivered by a data warehouse. A further dimension of the analytical process is that it is possible, based on the data warehouse information, to examine the development of customer segments. One potential analysis would be looking at which customer segments buy which products, as well as the development of these segments. This analysis can then be broken down on countries, chains, brands, and so on. Often businesses do not just sell one product or service per customer. Some software packages consist of a number of optional modules. Another example is car sales. Special rims cost extra, and the customer can choose not to buy them. Mobile subscriptions typically offer a large number of optional products, a guarantee never to have to pay more than a certain amount per month, favorite numbers that you can ring for less, insurance for the phone, and so forth. The analyst must not only compute the profitability of individual products, but also include any cross-sales related to the product.

If the assumption is that you are serving only one customer segment, you have several techniques to uncover customers' multiple-purchase patterns. Correlation analysis can use statistics to prove whether there are, between any two services on offer, any positive or negative purchasing tendencies, and thereby show whether the products are complementary or substituting. Principal component analyses (also known as PCA or explorative factor analysis) are able to provide information about how many multiple-purchase patterns there are as well as describe them. We are not looking only at whether products are sold in twos. A multiple-purchase pattern can include five products that are sold together.

If we are working with large numbers of different products (let's say more than 100), data mining techniques will start to become the most interesting ones. The methods are called everything from basket analysis to cross-sales analysis. The technique is based on uncovering which products are sold together. The underlying methodology is based on the same mind-set as a correlation analysis and involves a simple counting of how often two products are seen together as a multiple purchase on the same receipt or under the same customer number in the data warehouse.

The knowledge these analyses bring to the strategic planning process is the basic information that describes which products secure earnings (not revenue), and where investment in technology seems to be rendering a positive return estimated over the entire lifetime of the product.

When we begin to relate products to each other, knowledge is created about which basic needs we meet for our customers. Products are positioned in relation to each other, in connection with future marketing initiatives. If it's a matter of whether products can be integrated into each other, such as phones with cameras, GPS units and entertainment, or software packages such as Microsoft Office (spreadsheets, presentation programs, and word-processing programs), then these analyses also provide us with input for future product development.

Furthermore, these multiple-purchase patterns tell us something about our customers' needs and, as such, provide us with a basis for segmentation based on needs. Are our customers, for instance, buying large aluminum rims for their cars, or are they buying safety such as airbags and fire extinguishing equipment? The additional purchases meet different needs, which means that we should not be using the same sales strategies for all customers. So if a business is serving several segments, a cluster analysis is an obvious choice. Cluster analyses serve two purposes, first to identify how many segments a business is serving, and second to identify their characteristics. Whereas before it would make sense to discuss whether a multiple-purchase analysis is a natural part of strategy development, a cluster analysis would constitute a natural part of the identification and description of the customer groups a business is serving.

Once the segments are identified, we can compare their historic development with analyses of the future, and come up with estimates of what our customer mix will look like in the years ahead. Moreover, we will be able to estimate earnings from the different segments and in this way prepare strategic plans for who we want to serve in the future—and with which products and services.

Customer Relations Perspective

This perspective will typically be essential to enterprises with a focus on maintaining good customer relations. Banks, insurance companies, and telecoms, for instance, which are in markets with high degrees of penetration, are all good examples. Enterprises with a high degree of penetration must retain existing customers and at the same time attract customers from the competition. Their focus is customer loyalty. We will discuss this perspective in more detail in the CRM section of Chapter 3.

Other types of enterprises focus on using customer information actively as well. Examples are Apple, Nokia, Nike, and Coca-Cola. They usually have less transactional information about their customers than, say, banks, and the relationship is based to a lesser extent on a formal status, such as a subscription. The relationship is more of a psychological bond or a brand, if you will. A brand is used to wrap physical products in positive emotions to strengthen customer loyalty. These enterprises typically work with market information generated by "market intelligence." Information is typically collected for the occasion, often via external partners, competitor monitoring, and questionnaires. So it is not usually information stored in a data warehouse.

The big difference between the product perspective and the customer perspective is whether analyses are prepared based on products or customers. The analytical base table, which is the dataset underlying the analysis in its least aggregated form when looking at products, has as many rows as the business has active subscriptions. Further, their unique characteristic will, for instance, be their phone number. For the same telecom company, the analytical base table will have as many rows as the business has customers, if the analysis took its point of departure in the customer perspective. The difference here is that one customer may have several phone numbers. Just as we would group subscribers under a product name in connection with a product perspective, we would group customers in segments, if our base table were to support a customer perspective.

In other words, the enterprise needs to know which customers buy which products, to be able to prepare its analyses based on a customer perspective. If we imagine that we are a supermarket and the only electronic information we have is which products are sold together, we can prepare analyses based only on a product perspective, assuming we are working only with data warehouse information. This is why so many retail stores offer customer loyalty cards; it gives the business a possibility of carrying out analyses across several purchases in several stores linked via a customer code, which effectively makes the analysis customer oriented.

With an analytical base table, an obvious first exercise will be to perform a value-based segmentation. The result of such an analysis is a breakdown of customers in segments of gold, silver, and bronze or high, medium, and low. The breakdown is relevant because it forms the basis for how to treat customers. The most valuable customers must be retained, the middle ones must be grown via added sales activities, and the least valuable—who often cost the company—must not constitute an obstacle to other customers. Meanwhile, relationship costs to this group must be minimized. Strategically this analysis is central, too, as it is based on this information that the two most important objectives are to be defined. First, how big do we want the customer base to be by the end of next year, and second, how big must average sales be per customer, which is the income basis for a typical business?

Other types of segmentations that may be relevant in connection with strategic development processes are based on demand and behavior, respectively. These segmentations are prepared based on product information and transactions over time. They are typically performed for marketing purposes and are often supplemented by market analyses. They are, however, still essential in a strategic context, because they are the ones that tell the organization which trends are experienced in the marketplace. At the same time, the service offerings must be updated based on customer needs and adapted to the future, which is one of the important reasons for developing a strategy. Segmentation can, of course, also build on information about age, gender, geography, and education. But it is important to note that these so-called sociodemographics do not tell us anything about customer needs.

Only needs-based segmentation delivers this. When it has been performed, sociodemographics can be added to see what is characteristic of the individual segments. This enables the enterprise to ensure that the adopted method of communication to the various segments is appropriate. And this is the whole idea of segmentation, that is, to target marketing activities based on the disclosed needs of the segments, an action that delivers the opportunity to optimize the effect of every marketing dollar spent.

Customer lifetime value represents a new type of information that has great potential as a contributor to improved decision making at the strategic level. The concept originates from CRM and can be found by asking: "How much can I expect to earn from a given customer in the time he or she is with me?'" This can be calculated as:

Average earnings per month × number of months the customer
is with me ÷ the costs of obtaining the customer

So-called churn predictive decision trees can provide us with this exact information. These trees are based on data mining models, which can calculate the risk of each individual customer leaving a company. Based on these models, algorithms can be employed to divide the customer base into different groups based on whether they are going to leave the business within a given period of time. (We describe this technique in more detail in Chapter 4 in the section about data mining.) The gist is that an enterprise can use these models to determine the probability of a customer canceling his or her relationship with the enterprise with a certain percentage, which delivers information about a customer's life expectancy. We therefore know both the average income from and the life expectancy of the customer, and can make a rough estimate of the life expectancy value of the customer, by multiplying the two. With regard to the costs involved in getting the customer, we can choose not to take this into account, depending on whether we have this information on an individual level.

The result of this type of analysis is that your customers are divided into segments, with different customer life expectancy values.

In addition, the models can provide us with information about why certain segments decide to leave our business, teaching us a lot about the strengths and weaknesses of our enterprise. These analyses therefore tell us which customers are going to leave us as well as their value to us, and thus which customers we should actively try to retain.

The Operational Excellence Perspective

When an organization has a strong focus on operational excellence, it means it focuses on effective ways of producing and delivering services to its customers. If a business, for instance, has built its market position on being the cheapest, it stands to reason that intense focus will be on the optimization of internal processes.

Any organization will, of course, be trying to optimize its internal processes. This is a day-to-day management task. The real question is whether this constitutes a key competitive parameter for the enterprise.

Organizations for which the operational excellence approach makes sense are typically capital-heavy businesses with significant initial investments. This makes an efficient return on invested capital essential. A cement factory is a good example of an enterprise that is unlikely to be using a product leadership strategy, since the product cannot differentiate itself technologically. A customer intimacy strategy does not seem relevant either since the assumption here would be that the relations one manufacturer is able to establish can be matched by other manufacturers of cement. Therefore, if the cement factory is to secure its survival in the long run, it has got to create competitive advantages built on its ability to produce and deliver its products better than the competition. It makes sense, therefore, to invest in technology in terms of the optimization of internal processes—but this is not a product excellence strategy, because the products delivered by the factory do not differentiate themselves technologically.

Other enterprises will be competing on economies of scale. That is, businesses will be focusing on a positive spiral: The more you produce, the cheaper it gets. Then you sell more, and then you can produce more. Airlines, hotels, general logistics and production companies are all good examples of this business model. In this case, it is not just a question of efficient production, but of the rate of utilization of capacity having a positive, cumulative effect.

Finally, we often see operational excellence initiatives in businesses right after a merger. These are common in situations where you work in a targeted way to create synergies. Overall, we are talking about organizations that have cost control as a key competitive parameter and that use the operational excellence approach. Market developments are, naturally, a determining factor, too. In a declining market, a business will try to minimize loss, which means a strong focus on costs. It's said that everyone can survive in a growth market, but it is in a negative market that businesses must prove their worth, by retaining their equities and market share via an ongoing adaptation of internal processes. At a strategic level, we can work with two types of information. First, and most obvious, is the measuring of target achievement of internal process as a result of existing strategies. That will tell us where we are. Equally important is knowing where we should have been, and therefore where we need more resources or competencies or both. This is information that is essential in understanding the organization's weaknesses, and which can often be described in more detail in the internal analysis, where we look at whether all the parts of the organization are pulling in the same direction.

The other type of information we should focus on is the organization's key figures. All organizations have this information because it measures exactly what we are focusing on in relation to operational excellence—that is, how to optimize processes in order to minimize the consumption of resources without losing customer loyalty.

This is measurement by financial results that we can work to optimize; we can use the information to compare ourselves with the external accounts of competing enterprises. This, of course, is of great interest when competing on price, as it is the underlying cost structure that shows our competitors' strong and weak points in this kind of competitive situation. On BA-support.com, we have entered a large number of key indicators along with directions about how to compute them and subsequently interpret them.

At an operational level you will typically find that process owners use tools like control charts and other Six Sigma or lean tools. The overall purpose is to minimize waste and variance in internal processes by making the processes stable and predictable, because those are the cheapest processes to manage from a performance management perspective. After all, it is only unstable and unpredictable processes that generate waste in terms of overwork, large inventories, and unexpected waiting time between process steps.

SUMMARY

In this chapter, we looked at different degrees of integration between the strategy and BA functions. No degree or level of integration is more correct than any other. It all depends on the organization's strategy, internal competencies, technological options, and competitive situation. You will be able to assess the level of integration between the two in your own organization and decide whether the actual level corresponds with the strategic level as well as whether the strategic level uses the full potential of information as a strategic resource.

The scenarios began with a lack of integration, which means that the BA function is not formally perceived as part of the strategy development process, and is therefore solely operating on an ad hoc basis—if indeed there is a BA function at all. The second scenario has the BA function in a purely reactive role in relation to the strategy function.

This means that objectives are specified for the rest of the organization, but that there is no feedback procedure from BA to strategy, in case there are significant deviations from meeting objectives at a functional level. The third scenario is characterized by a formalized feedback procedure from the BA function to the strategy function. This means that formalized procedures must be introduced to analyze target achievement on an ongoing basis to improve performance in individual departments, but also with the purpose of generating knowledge about the scope for strategic improvement. Finally, we presented a scenario in which information is perceived and used as a strategic resource. This requires that the people responsible for strategy formulation understand the competitive opportunities that can be derived from this information. Since strategic opportunities also depend on the way in which a business has decided to compete, we introduced a method to help you identify the relationship between your own competitive disciplines and the potentially most relevant information.

Three competitive disciplines were introduced. The first was product innovation. Business analytics can deliver information about which products create the business's income over its entire lifetime. In addition, BA can provide the organization with information about which product attributes it would be relevant to develop for which customer segments. The second competitive discipline was about strong customer relations, where BA can provide answers to the business about how to compose and develop individualized loyalty and income-generating customer programs. The third competitive discipline was the operational excellence approach, where BA can provide the business with information and knowledge about which of its processes to strengthen and develop in relation to its own requirements and in relation to the strengths of the competition.

CHAPTER **3**

Development and Deployment of Information at the Functional Level

usiness analytics (BA) creates value only if operational processes
are improved or if new ones are initiated. Your lead information
is used to improve existing processes or initiate completely new
business processes. Your lag information is used to measure existing
processes, typically via key performance indicators (KPIs). In this
chapter, we look at the second of the five levels in the BA model introduced in Chapter 1. At this level, we identify how to get from having
some overall objectives for a department to being able to specify the
information requirements. We discuss the relationship between BA
and the operational level and the relationship between strategic plans
and how to operationalize them with a focus on the BA function's
deliveries.

So what we do is to specify which information we need in order to
implement the objectives we have been given as a department, based
on the corporate strategy from the last chapter. Another way of describing this is to talk about developing an information strategy,

EXHIBIT 3.1 From Overall Strategy to Information Requirements at a Functional Level

because just as we need to formulate a customer relationship management (CRM) strategy to reflect the overall strategy and its requirements to the CRM function, we also need to have an information strategy in place that reflects the requirements of the corporate strategy to BA. The relationship is illustrated in Exhibit 3.1, which is an elaboration of Exhibit 2.3. In order to show the relationship between this chapter and the previous one, we have indicated in the model how the corporate strategy is presented in objectives to be met by the individual functions. Each of these departments within the organization then needs to develop a function strategy with subsequent information requirements.

This chapter takes its theoretical point of departure in a Rockart model, which is used to establish new business processes. We will go through the model, and then present an example of how to employ it in practice in connection with the establishment of new processes in a CRM department. We have chosen this particular example because it is based on customer information that, on the one hand is stored in many data warehouses, and that, on the other hand, can be difficult to derive the full value from simply because there is so much of it. Often, a business will find itself in the bizarre situation of almost drowning in data, while the organization thirsts for information and knowledge. Now that we've got all this information in a central data warehouse, how do we get value out of it?

Later on in the chapter we'll take a closer look at how to monitor and improve operational processes with performance management, using, among other things, an example from a call center. This example focuses more on optimizing operational processes that are already established. This means that lead information is created on the basis of analyses of the lag information of the process, which in turn means that learning loops are established. We offer eleven suggestions for processes, which could constitute initial areas for optimization. Finally, we list a number of KPIs to use at a functional level. They do not represent an answer book as such, but may provide you with inspiration and work to bring the theories down to earth.

In this chapter, we also introduce the concepts of lead and lag information, where *lead* represents something that comes before, and *lag* describes something that comes after. We include these terms because we're taking our point of departure in a process perspective, where lead describes the information or the knowledge necessary for getting started in the first place with a new process or improving an existing one. The opposite is lag information, which is about the continuous measuring of how the process is developing. The purpose of lag information is, therefore, to monitor whether we are meeting our objectives or whether we need to make some adjustments. This information also works as input to analyses of the relationship between the actions we take as an organization, and the specific and measurable results these actions achieve. In other words, we are talking about proactive knowledge or information to be used to create new processes and reactive information, which monitors processes that are already up and running.

Lead information is therefore more abstract and will typically be knowledge that is imparted on the basis of ad hoc projects. By contrast, lag information often is conventionally automated reporting on key indicators, which indicate whether the process is meeting its specified objectives. The relationship between lead and lag information will be discussed further later on in this chapter.

After you read this chapter, you will understand which knowledge and information are needed based on a given department strategy. You can then proceed to Chapter 4, which describes the analytical level of the model. This is where we define specific methods in statistics, data mining, and reporting, in order to show how the required knowledge and information are delivered in a format that is tailored to meet the needs of the department's strategy. The link between this chapter and the next is that in this chapter we define which information we need based on the overall corporate strategy, and in the next chapter we look at how this information can be created. Together, these constitute an information strategy.

The following case study introduces key concepts in BA at an operational level.

CASE STUDY: A TRIP TO THE SUMMERHOUSE

We will draw on this example throughout this chapter, introducing concepts such as KPIs, performance management (also called corporate performance management [CPM] and business performance management [BPM]), lead information (information for Business process reengeneering), lag information (information for monitoring of processes), and the definition of information requirements based on critical success factors (lead and lag information combined) and dashboards (a tool for monitoring the organization's processes). So lean back—you're going on a trip to the summerhouse. The route we're taking is 60 miles long and is expected to take 60 minutes. As we continue, you will monitor and measure the operational process that is required to take this trip. From a business perspective, you are looking for answers to three questions; your BA function must answer them.

1. **Status:** "Have I gone far enough in relation to how long I've been on the road?"

2. **Trend:** "Am I accelerating up or down, or is my speed constant?"

3. **Projection:** "Given my speed and how far I've gone, will I reach the summerhouse at the expected time?"

Specification of Requirements

You can now start making your specification of requirements for your performance management dashboard. Your goal is to drive 60 miles in 60 minutes. You can now also place in your budget a goal line as shown in Exhibit 3.2, which is a straight line and a function of time. In other words, you choose a goal that is to drive with the same speed all the way. To do that, you must be halfway through after 30 minutes.

Your KPI must specify key elements of your performance and give you an idea of the degree of success with your project. An obvious choice of KPI will therefore be the relationship between what you have achieved and what you plan to achieve.

Your KPI = Actual miles/Budgeted miles (specified goal)

Visually, this means that the graph with actual miles is lying above the budget curve, when your KPI is more than 1. (See Exhibit 3.2.)

In addition to the graph, you could set up a "cockpit" or performance management dashboard, consisting of a number of simple indicators for the process. Here we have made a status indicator showing your current KPI, and this is more than 1 when the status line is over our budget line.

We have also added a trend meter, which points downward if the speed in the current period is lower than the speed in the previous period. The situation at the black dot in Exhibit 3.2 is therefore that

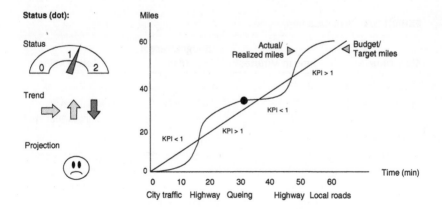

EXHIBIT 3.2 Example of a Performance Management Dashboard for the Trip

we are doing well overall, but that we should be aware that we are losing speed. Further, we have added a smiley face on this dashboard with information about whether the summerhouse will be reached on time given the current location and acceleration. This last KPI is illustrated by a smiley that is happy, neutral or unhappy, depending on a projection of whether we will reach our destination on time, might reach our destination on time, or won't reach our destination on time, based on current statuses. At an overall level, we just have to keep an eye on the smiley.

Your Technical Support

So what do you need in terms of technical support to realize this specification of requirements? Exhibit 3.3 shows a section of your base table.

Your data in the start time, budget, and time columns is fixed before you begin your trip. These values are static. The column with actually driven miles is updated on an ongoing basis by program code that reads the number of driven miles. A new figure is added to the table in the column with actual miles every minute. Then the graphics on your data-driven and dynamic dashboard are updated. All the data in the table is read every minute to the graphical object that shows the curve and actual and expected miles. Then your KPI is computed by dividing the latest number of actual miles by the number of expected

EXHIBIT 3.3 Your Base Table

Start Time	Time in Minutes	Budget/Target Miles	Actual Miles
14.32 - 20 Feb 10	0	0	0
14.32 - 20 Feb 10	1	1.00 (60/60)	? (not known till 1 minute after start)
14.32 - 20 Feb 10	–		–
14.32 - 20 Feb 10	59	59.00 (1.00 × 59)	60.00 –(I reach my target after 59 minutes)
14.32 - 20 Feb 10	60	60 (1.00 × 60)	?

budget miles, and the change can be seen in real time on your dashboard, along with any replaced GIF arrow (graphic image of an arrow) and smiley. If you drove faster in the previous minute (actual miles/time) compared to the minute before, the GIF arrow pointing upwards is loaded. If the latest KPI is computed to be more than 1, the happy smiley is loaded for your performance dashboard in Exhibit 3.2.

And Now Off We Go to the Summerhouse

You start your journey, and the first couple of points on your status curve in Exhibit 3.2 appear on your dashboard after a minute, along with your other graphics. You're driving in the city and are therefore under the budget line. Your KPI is under 1 and your smiley is unhappy. Your trend arrow, however, is pointing upwards most of the time, as you slowly, minute by minute, increase your speed on your way out of the city. Your performance monitoring encourages you to drive faster, but that just won't do on city roads—and you do find that annoying! Once on the highway you finally get over the budget line and your KPI is now over 1. Your smiley becomes neutral and then happy and the trend arrow is still pointing upwards, as you continue to increase your speed. Then you run into traffic on the interstate. Your KPI falls back through 1, as you're now getting under the budget line. Your smiley is unhappy and your trend arrow begins to point straight ahead, as you're having to stop the car!

However, the traffic quickly dissolves, and you increase speed significantly to get to your summerhouse on time. Your KPI goes from 0.9 and breaks through 1. Your smiley is happy again (just like you) and your trend arrow has pointed upwards ever since the traffic became lighter. When after a while you leave the highway, your KPI is 1.1 (10% over target or budget). The last bit of the trip, you'll be driving on smaller roads and your speed will therefore fall. Your trend arrow points downwards, your status speedometer slowly drops towards 1. But you're feeling optimistic, because you know that you've got enough margin for the last part of the trip, as your smiley and KPI both show you.

By means of the above example, we've tried to illustrate the idea behind KPIs and performance management. The example may seem trivial, but it does provide a useful insight into key concepts and how to monitor a business process.

Your Lead and Lag information

The summerhouse example also gives us an understanding of the two types of information used by the BA function—lead and lag information.

Lag information is retrospective information, which we choose to register on an ongoing basis in our data warehouse in connection with performance management. In the summerhouse example the lag information is the actual number of miles. Lag information is typically stored in tables in the business's data warehouse and is used for analyses to create a learning loop back to the strategy (see Chapter 2 on strategy) or for new lead information.

Lead information has a completely different character than lag information. Lead information is used to improve existing business processes or initiate ones. Lead information in the BA framework is typically created on the basis of an analysis of lag information and is therefore usually not stored in tables, since this information, as already mentioned, is the outcome of an analytical process. Lead information will typically have the character of "breaking insight," which can be used to improve overall business processes, and provide learning loops back to the strategic level. An analytical process using, for instance, a data mining methodology on your base table in Exhibit 3.3 (naturally, after you've done the trip to the summerhouse several times) would be a useful tool for the uncovering of key factors to provide you with knowledge about why you tend to arrive at the summerhouse early (KPI > 1) or late (KPI < 1). This hopefully statistically significant knowledge about the correlation will, in future, help you arrive at your target on time and thereby achieve success. Your breaking insight, which is the outcome of these analytical processes on your historical data, could be a statistically significant correlation between the value of your KPI, when you reach your target, and the start time of your journey. The correlation is illustrated in Exhibit 3.4.

You will usually have a successful trip to the summerhouse if you start your driving before 2 PM or after 7 PM (KPI > 1). The worst time to

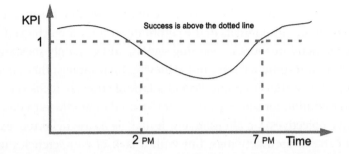

EXHIBIT 3.4 Analytical Outcome of the Correlation between Your End KPI and Start Time of Journey

start is between 4 PM and 5 PM. If you start within this time interval, your chances of reaching your target on time are minimal. The explanation is, of course, that it takes longer to get through the city in rush hour traffic, and you'll almost always end up queuing on the motorway. Your breaking insight or lead information, which we could also call your critical success factor, will be: You must start your trip to the summerhouse before 2 PM or after 7 PM in order to optimize/improve your operational process and be successful in your endeavor.

Note that the new important lead information identified by analytics obviously works to provide a learning loop back to the strategic level (see Chapter 2) to be used next time a strategy is developed for the coming year. In this section, we'll take a closer look at what KPIs are, how they are generated, and what they can be used for. The creation of KPIs is normally intuitive as illustrated in the above summerhouse example.

Generally speaking, KPIs describe the relationship between the organization's activities and its financial targets. KPIs can be financial key indicators or index figures specified for the occasion. What is required of them is simply that they, on the one hand, set some standards for how business processes must perform (lag information) and on the other define which activities have "gone wrong," if the process does not meet its objectives (define causal relations). This means that if we have a KPI, and we are below target, we always know which consequences this will have in the long run. We know which activities may influence it indirectly by influencing the process it is measuring.

This knowledge enables us to adjust activities and thereby ensure that the overall financial targets in the corporate strategy are achieved.

KPIs therefore work as warning signals, and generally speaking we can say that if some KPIs are not achieving their targets, there may be two reasons. Either it's a question of a lack of strategic focus (i.e., that the organization for some reason is not focused in its efforts to meet the strategic objectives) or, alternatively, it may be a case of correct execution of the desired activities, but with a lack of competencies or resources, which means that the activities do not reach the desired level.

Another important function of KPIs is that they are able to stop activities again. It is not uncommon for CRM departments to have to take on many troubleshooting tasks. When you face a problem, you solve it by starting a new and corrective process. But when do you stop these processes again? If you fail to do so, the organization's CRM strategy will become a patchwork quilt of historical troubleshooting exercises. If you are constantly patching things up, more and more resources will be needed over time to maintain these stopgap measures throughout the organization. When systematically collected, KPIs also provide the organization with a memory, which means that learning can be derived from successful projects. This learning may come by means of analytics, which we will cover in the following section, but also by holding people to their promises. It is quite a common phenomenon to have people who are extremely good at convincing management that they have a great idea for a campaign. And then there are people who make great campaigns. As the two are not necessarily the same, measuring KPIs will tell the organization whether campaigns are working. In the long run, this means that you get an organization where the focus is on results, rather than on what sells internally.

More about Lead and Lag Information

As mentioned in the introduction and in the summerhouse example, BA often distinguishes between lead and lag information, where *lead information* is the knowledge we need to initiate or improve a process. If we take our point of departure in our trip to the summerhouse, there are two possibilities; either it's our first trip there on that route, or we've gone that way before.

If it's our first time on that route, we must initiate a new process, because we're doing something for the first time. This also means that we have no historical knowledge about how long it takes to take that route, and we therefore have to plan our trip based on other information, such as directions from the Internet or general experience with how long that kind of trip takes. What we're talking about here is *lead information*, the information that will get us to the summerhouse using the correct route with arrival on the correct time. Therefore it is information that we need to have, before we start our trip.

As we are driving toward the summerhouse, we receive a large amount of lag information. The nature of lag information is that it monitors our process. We can react to it and adjust our actions by driving faster or slower, but it will not change the actual process we are in, based on this information. This is information we collect and use in the course of the process.

If we get fed up with the route we've chosen and want to find a new one, we have to start looking for new lead information to find out whether there is another route that may be quicker and easier. If we then choose to go by the new route, we will again be generating lag information, based on which we will create expectations to whether we reach the summerhouse on time. If it is not the first time we take the given route to the summerhouse, we already have knowledge about the usual course of the trip. We have, in other words, lag information telling us how long the trip usually takes, whether the traffic is different at different times of the day, week, and year. Based on the lag information we're already in possession of, we can generate new lead information because we know when we want to reach the summerhouse, and how the traffic usually is at the given time. We can therefore count back and find out when we need to leave, and plan whether there is time for other activities before we go. We can, in other words, learn from our internal knowledge and optimize the process, which is the trip to the summerhouse. This is exactly what we do in connection with process optimization, where we are not just using lag information to monitor whether the process meets its objectives. Rather, we are also saving this lag information for future analyses to improve this process via lead information that has the character of being breaking insight.

Since the subject of this book is how to optimize business processes based on strategic requirements, we have chosen to include two perspectives. One perspective is the establishment of a process for the first time, which includes identifying which lead and lag information is required in the organization, so that we can initiate and manage the given process.

The second perspective is taking its point of departure in a strategic demand for the optimization of given business processes. Since this process is already established, we can use saved lag information describing the correlation between the process, the way in which it has been influenced and the effect it had on the process, and derive knowledge about how we can optimize the process. So, based on lag information, we can generate lead information, and if the nature of the process is not being completely restructured based on learning from the new lead information, this learning cycle can be maintained.

In terms of our trip to the summerhouse, we can continue to cut back on minutes and seconds of the drive while potentially minimizing petrol consumption, if we measure that, too, and thereby improve our process on an ongoing basis. This is a case of optimizing processes by improving the use of resources (less petrol consumption, for instance, if you observe traffic regulations and do a bit of shopping, which should otherwise have been done separately) and optimized user satisfaction with the process (the fact that we arrive exactly on time without stressing, and maybe get out and stretch our legs on the way, if that is what the users ask for at the beginning). The reason for separating the two is the fact that passengers in the car don't always want to get out to shop, or start the trip early and do 50 miles per hour to minimize fuel consumption. Passengers are not likely, either, to appreciate the excellent service it would have been, if you could get them to the summerhouse in half the normal time by doing 160 miles per hour. The same thing occurs in a restaurant where service has been cut back too much or the level of service has been raised so high you don't want to pay for it. The way to optimize resources in a business process has got to take user satisfaction into consideration, which is a fundamental rule in performance management.

ESTABLISHING BUSINESS PROCESSES
WITH THE ROCKART MODEL

The model we're using in this section is strongly influenced by the so-called critical success factor model, and we use it to describe the relationship between the objectives as defined at the strategic level and the new processes with the subsequent information needs. As discussed in Chapter 2, the annual strategy development process results in a number of objectives formulated by the organization's strategic level, which are then communicated to the operational level of the business. To meet these objectives, the individual department must make a plan for its actions in the coming period. We will call this plan a strategy, too, only it is developed at an operational level and is a result of the overall corporate strategy. These strategies will therefore be called CRM strategy, human resources strategy, BA strategy, logistics strategy, inventory strategy, and so on, depending on which department they belong to. (See Exhibit 3.5.)

On the basis of its local strategy, the department must identify the critical success factors, which are the elements of the plan that must have a successful outcome, if the plan as a whole is to succeed. If you are building a sales department it will therefore be a critical success factor that you are able to attract good salespeople; or if you want to carry out successful system implementation, the requirements will be that users take to it, and that the system is user-friendly, and that the data quality, for instance, is high, too. It is important to note that if just one of the critical success factors fails, the whole strategy is expected to fail, which means that our specified objectives are not met. We normally expect between three and five critical success factors, but there may, of course, be huge deviations from this, depending on the extent of the strategy, its complexity, and so forth.

Based on the critical success factors, the BA function will be asked to deliver various types of information. Generally speaking, we can expect to be asked to deliver lag information to enable the process owners to monitor whether the new sales department is coming up with the required results. Sometimes the BA function will be asked to deliver lead information, too. For example, if we, as in the following

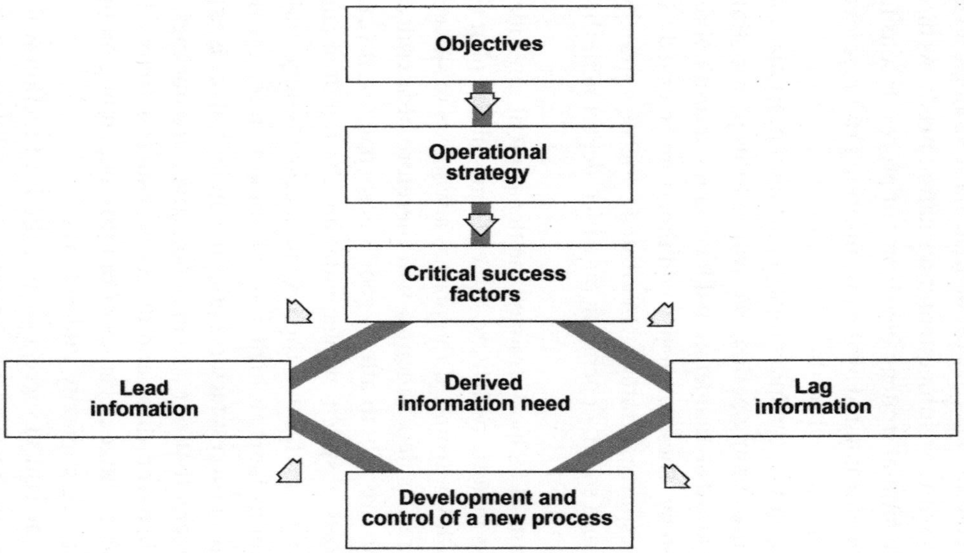
Objectives
Operational strategy
Critical success factors
Derived information need
Lead infomation
Lag information
Development and control of a new process

EXHIBIT 3.5 From Departmental Objectives to the Development of a New Process

example, are carrying out a sales campaign targeted toward our existing customer base, we might be asked to deliver information about which customers, based on consumption profiles, can be expected to be interested in which offers. In other cases, such as the establishment of a new sales department, the BA function may be able to deliver information about what a "good" salesperson normally looks like based on human resources information. Sometimes the BA function will not be able to deliver the desired knowledge, and then the process owner will have to get this knowledge from somewhere else. As the example shows, the BA function will almost always be asked to deliver lag information in connection with major strategic projects. The question is whether the BA function can or will be asked to deliver lead information in connection with the establishment of new processes.

EXAMPLE: ESTABLISHING NEW BUSINESS PROCESSES WITH THE ROCKART MODEL

Your lead information or breaking insight, which we could also call your critical success factor, is the information based on analytics that will allow your business to go beyond traditional business intelligence reporting and into the future using information as a strategic resource.

Level 1: Identifying the Objectives

Imagine that you work in the marketing department of a large telecom enterprise. A marketing department has two overall purposes: to attract new customers via campaigns on television, in magazines, and other media, and to hold on to the existing customers.

In order to achieve good customer relations, many businesses adopt dialogue programs, which inform customers of new prices, stores, products, and so forth. Some of this communication has the purpose of educating the customer, but most of the communication is aimed at expanding and strengthening the customer's involvement. If, for instance, a customer has a mobile phone, we could train them in using MMS or surfing the Internet via the phone, and thereby create higher income per customer. Another way of expanding a customer's involvement is to make sure he or she does not jump ship and join the competition. Finally, you must imagine that this is December and that your boss has just given you next year's target for your department. (See Exhibit 3.6.)

The targets are: At the end of the year, the telecom company's customer base must be 10% bigger and the average income per customer must have gone up by 10%.

Level 2: Identifying an Operational Strategy

Since you are responsible for CRM and you now know your targets, this means that the strategy must be based on the creation of growth in your customer base by becoming better at holding on to them. As the one who is responsible for CRM, you know that you if can hold on to your most valuable customers, average income will go up as a result of a more valuable customer portfolio. You therefore decide, as a starting point, to concentrate on retaining the most valuable third of your customer base. This is based on the fact that the company has already performed a value-based segmentation, dividing its customers into gold, silver, and bronze customers, and that each of these segments constitutes about a third. Based on this, it is relatively easy for you to determine the average value of the customer base, if you were to add the additional 10% gold customers, as is your intention. After some calculations, you find that if your gold customers grow by 10%, your average revenue per customer will go up by 5%. As the average market growth is 3%, you still need a strategy for how to create growth in the average revenue per customer of the remaining 2%. You decide to create the 2% via added sales to your existing customers.

As illustrated by Exhibit 3.7, you now have a two-part strategy: Retain your gold customers and initiate added sales activities to your customer base.

Level 3: Identifying the Critical Success Factors

Defining the critical success factors before starting on a project is always subject to discussion, a discussion that may still be going

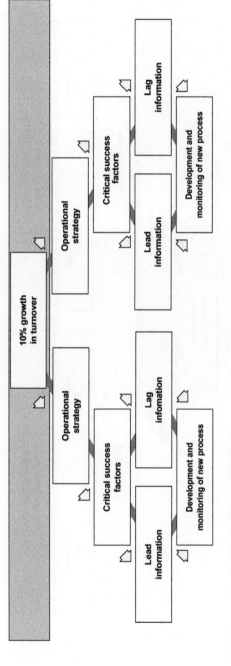

EXHIBIT 3.6 Level 1: Identification of Objectives

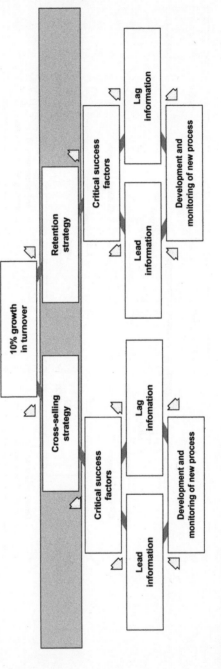

EXHIBIT 3.7 Level 2: Identifying an Operational Strategy

on throughout the project. In this context, we take the BA perspective and focus only on what may be of importance to our information strategy.

This step in the process toward an information strategy is based on the fact that when you implement a strategy, you initiate a large number of activities, and some of these activities are more critical than others. It is, for example, key to your retention activities that you find out why customers leave your company, and that you develop retention offers that are at least as good as those of your competitors.

In addition to this, your budgets tell you that you cannot afford to send out valuable retention offers to all of your 100,000 gold customers. It is, therefore, essential to your CRM strategy that you obtain knowledge about which customers intend to leave, when, and why. With that knowledge you have only to contact customers who are likely to leave you. You want information about when you need to contact this group of customers, as well as knowledge about which offer you must give the individual customer. If you hold in one hand the knowledge about which of your customers intend to leave you, and in the other an effective retention offer, then you have some excellent tools for carrying out your retention campaign. It is therefore a critical success factor that you can offer the right customers the right retention offers at the right time. Otherwise your retention campaign will fail.

It is the same thing with your cross-sell activities. You want to communicate only offers that your customers will be interested in. For example, you don't want to spend resources promoting the use of short message service (SMS) to your fixed line customers, because they'll ignore it at best. At worst, they'll be annoyed that they as your customers are paying for and spending time on misplaced letters.

It is therefore a critical success factor for your cross-sell activities that you know which customers can be assumed to be interested in your various added sales offers. In other words, it is a critical success factor for your cross-sell campaign that you are able to give the right customers the right offer at the right time. Otherwise your added sales campaign will fail. (See Exhibit 3.8.)

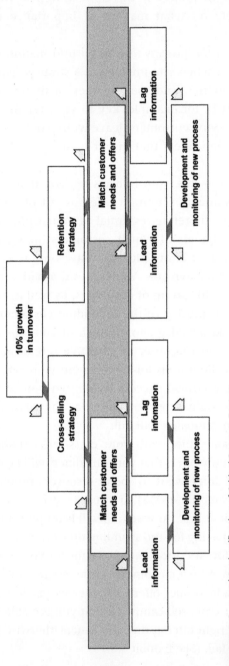

EXHIBIT 3.8 Level 3: Identification of Critical Success Factors

Level 4: Identifying Lead and Lag Information

So the knowledge you're after in connection with your customer retention strategy must answer the question: Which customers are leaving me, when, and why? Once you've got that knowledge, you can carry out campaigns with the right retention offer for the right customers at the right time. At the same time, you want to fulfill your added sales strategy. You want to know which customers will buy what and when.

All this is lead information. In other words, it is information or knowledge that is necessary for even beginning your new business activities. You also want to collect lag information because it's important to be able to monitor the processes to see whether you are going to fulfill your strategies. If it looks as if that will not be the case, you want to be able to act as quickly as possible to make adjustments.

You therefore want to receive information on an ongoing basis about how the individual campaigns are going. Are there some of them, for instance, that are doing better than expected and which could therefore be rolled out further, or are there some that should be cancelled altogether? Of course, you also want to receive continuous information about the size of your customer base along with the average income per customer. All this is summarized in Exhibit 3.9.

In Exhibit 3.10, we illustrated lead and lag information seen from a process perspective. We want to repeat that lead information does not necessarily have to come solely from the BA function. It just does in this example. There will be cases where the BA function is unable to support the decisions, for if there is no relevant information to support the solution of the problem in the existing data warehouse, there is no point in involving conventional data warehouse analysts as part of the project. To further exemplify the difference between initiating new processes and monitoring existing ones, it is said rather wryly in controller/accountancy environments "possibly the most valuable person in the entire organization is the one who is able to start up new and relevant business initiatives (via lead information). But the second most valuable person in the organization is without a doubt the one who is able to stop all the wrong initiatives (via lag information which the controllers themselves are managing)."

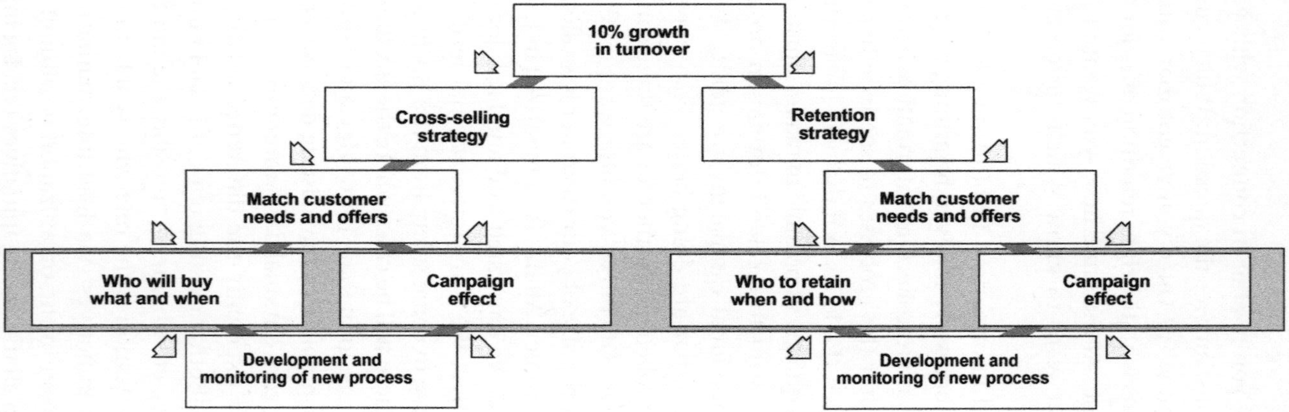

10% growth in turnover
Cross-selling strategy
Retention strategy
Match customer needs and offers
Match customer needs and offers
Who will buy what and when
Campaign effect
Who to retain when and how
Campaign effect
Development and monitoring of new process
Development and monitoring of new process

EXHIBIT 3.9 Level 4: Identifying Critical Success Factors

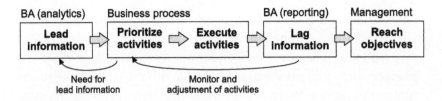

EXHIBIT 3.10 Level 5: Using Lead and Lag Information in Relation to the Development and Management of a Business Process

Your department can now carry out the new business initiatives, and the BA function can support with lag information that informs you on an ongoing basis about whether the process is meeting the defined objectives. This information is typically delivered as conventional KPIs to management and process owners, more frequently and in more depth than lead information.

For details about how to generate information about which customers will leave you, when, and why, see the data mining section of Chapter 4. Here we will explain decision trees. These trees show us, customer by customer, which risk there is of him or her cancelling their customer relationship in the coming period of time. In addition to this, the trees enable us to interpret the reason behind the given risk profile, and thus also what can be done to retain the customer.

In the section about data mining, we will also be looking at cross-sales models, which identify consumer patterns based on historical information. Based on these, we will suggest, for each individual customer, what he or she should be offered and when. Finally, you can visit the Web site BA-support.com, where you'll find a case study that describes how one telecom company, via business intelligence (BI)-driven CRM strategy, went from a deficit of $40 million at the end of 2004 to a profit of $60 million the following year. In that case, data mining was a driving force for the entire project.

OPTIMIZING EXISTING BUSINESS PROCESSES

In the previous section, we discussed how the BA function can support the establishment of new business processes by delivering lag information and, in some cases, by delivering lead information. When you're working with the optimization of existing processes, you can save lag information over time and thus create data for analysis that produces new lead information (breaking insights) as we saw in the summerhouse case study. It goes without saying, that if lag information is not saved over time, there will be no information to analyze. BA–driven optimization of existing process is therefore about turning your lag information into lead information.

If you introduce new bonus programs for your salespeople, will they sell more? And what is the optimum balance between fixed salary and target salary? If we train our call center employees, will this have a positive effect on their performance? And what is that worth in terms of money, and which kind of training will give us the best result? Key performance indicators can, in other words, show us the correlations between the process-improving activities that we carry out, their effect on the process and the individual process owners' KPIs and, finally, tell us whether the activities are worth the cost. All this is summarized in Exhibit 3.11.

In this context, it is worth emphasizing that we are talking about indicators, as it is impossible to measure all aspects of a process. We therefore choose a few and telling ones that we can relate to the strategic objectives at an operational level, as we've seen in the previous Critical Success Factor model.

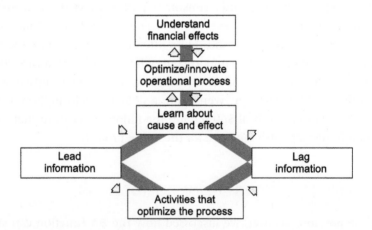

EXHIBIT 3.11 Optimization of Existing Processes

EXAMPLE: DEPLOYING PERFORMANCE MANAGEMENT TO OPTIMIZE EXISTING PROCESSES

The example with a trip to the summerhouse illustrated some relations between KPIs and derived activities. In performance management, however, the world is a bit more complicated. Which accelerator should we press if customers are unhappy with the service they receive from a call center? How hard and how long should we be pressing the accelerator, and when can we expect to see the effect of our pressing the accelerator?

The next example is therefore different from the trip to the summerhouse example because we're introducing more layers of KPIs to enable us to monitor correlations between initiated activities all the way to the strategic and financial objectives they must fulfill. The example also deviates from the CRM example in that we're not creating new processes, but rather working with the optimization of existing ones. In the CRM case study, we were project-oriented. By that we mean that we wanted to carry out some campaigns, and monitor our lag information, whether we reached our target. When the campaigns were done, we didn't look at doing any further work with the lag information. In the next example, our work will be more process-oriented, so we will work with the optimization of business procedures that are already established. From a purely practical point of view, this means that we'll be focusing more on the lag information by collecting and analyzing it to understand correlations and thereby to be able to further improve processes in the future. So we're not just using lag information as KPIs to see whether our processes are on track. Instead, we're systematically collecting lag information in a data warehouse, because we want to use it later to generate lead information.

Concept of Performance Management

First and foremost, however, we want to introduce the concept of performance management and what it covers. Very briefly, it can be described as the optimization of processes. As a point of departure, a process can be optimized in two ways. First, by ensuring a better use of resources deployed in keeping the process going. Second, by improving the result of what comes out of the process. This is also the essence of what is known to some as Lean, where we try to reduce waste in our processes, or Six Sigma, where we to a larger extent seek to minimize the variation in our processes in order to make better use of our resources and provide our process users with a better output.

Being focused on the optimization of a process does not mean that the strategy is irrelevant, because the requirement for an optimization might well be derived from the strategy. Besides, strategy will always restrict our scope for what we can implement. If, for instance, we are an organization that competes on good service, there is a limit to how long we can let our customers wait when they call us. Firing some of the staff in the call center might be an easy way of saving money, but it would create an imbalance in relation to customer expectations. This balancing is at the very core of performance management (i.e., the optimum weighting of the resources that are used in a process in relation to the expected outcome of the process). In this call center example, you can cut back on staff to the extent that you are making your customers unhappy. On the other hand, a time will come when the number of staff is so high with costs to match that customers do not notice the difference and do not appreciate the increased costs, which ultimately they'll be paying. It's important to acknowledge, too, that good service is an expected quantity. On the one hand, we expect to be queuing at the post office and the discount store, but on the other we would find it unacceptable to have to queue for an ambulance after a traffic accident.

In the example, we must imagine that in connection with the telecom company's strategy two requirements have been put to the organization. The first is that the CRM department has interviewed customers who have cancelled their mobile phone subscription. Based on these interviews, it was found that a large number of the customers are dissatisfied with the service they received from the call center because they had to ring in several times to get a problem solved.

The other strategic requirement to the organization is that the call center needs to reduce its overall costs by 10%, without compromising the level of service given to customers. The strategy function has computed that if the two initiatives are successful, they will contribute significantly to the bottom line. The reason for this is that it is expensive to acquire new customers, because they must be given financial incentives, they incur initial set-up costs, and because bonuses must be paid to the stores that land these new customers. All in all, the cost of landing a new mobile phone customer is approximately U.S. $400 in Denmark at the time of writing. That is money that is wasted if the customer cancels his or her subscription, and that you must then reinvest in order to maintain the company's market share. The choice of the call center as an area to save money is based on the fact that it is a salary-heavy department, and it is thought that there is room for improvement in this area.

So imagine in this example that you're working with a call center in a telecom company. The purpose of a call center is to deal with incoming calls from customers as well as to make calls to customers. Incoming calls are generated by customers who have questions or want something done. This may concern their bills, setting up their mobile phones, or subscription cancellation. Outgoing calls may be concerned with campaign offers or the answers to questions that couldn't be answered when the customer called.

If we take a closer look at the process for incoming calls, they start with a customer ringing the call center. He or she might be waiting in a queue and subsequently transferred to an agent. The agent then needs to clarify the nature of the customer's request or problem, and then deal with it. The customer is then expected to hang up, and the request/problem is expected to have been met or solved. During the entire process, an automatic logging is performed. It records the time of the call and which phone number called in. The agent also logs what the problem is, and whether it has been solved, or whether someone else must get back to the customer later.

Sometimes when a customer calls to get a problem solved, this has not been possible. This is clear if the same customer calls back soon after with the same problem, and the agent then has to deal with the customer again. This has two consequences. One is that further resources are used to deal with a "repeat call" and another is that there will be a customer who is not satisfied with the advice received to begin with. If we are therefore looking at optimizing our process, we are presented with an opportunity to minimize the resource input and optimize customer satisfaction, if we can minimize the number of repeat calls.

In order to reduce the number of repeat calls, we need to obtain some information: Which agents generate many repeat calls and in connection with which problems? With this knowledge we know who to train and in what. To be able to measure the number of repeat calls, we must define it as a KPI. We also need to set a goal for the KPI, which could be a 20% reduction, to be able to achieve both strategic targets. We won't discuss why we've set the goal at 20%, and not more or less. Let's just assume the figure is an estimate based on various calculations.

We can turn the number of repeat calls into a KPI because we know which phone numbers ring in at which time and with which problems. We can therefore define a repeat call as having happened if the same phone number rings in with the same problem within one week. We are assuming that the problem was not solved in the course of the initial call. We also know which agent did not solve the problem the first time around so we can connect a name to the event. We will also make a measuring point: How many calls does this agent take on an average basis per hour? This is because the total number of customer problems that are dealt with must not drop as a result of our future activities.

In a couple of days' time, an analyst can now produce two types of reports, which will constitute our lead information. One report will focus on which types of problems typically generate repeat calls. Is there a specific type of problem that is generally difficult to solve? If this is the case, we can train all staff in how to solve these, and update internal manuals. The other report focuses on which agents generate many repeat calls. The recipient of the report is the team manager and agent himself, so that an individual training program can be set up. To motivate the agents, a bonus program is introduced that rewards staff who generate relatively few repeat calls, while still dealing with relatively many incoming calls.

As is illustrated by Exhibit 3.12, we have now established a considerable number of measuring points and related them to each other. We'll start with some of the activities at the bottom of the model, which are built on employee interviews, training, and bonus systems. These activities influence subsequent processes. The improved processes mean that not only is the call center making better use of its

		Lead/analysis and lag/goal information
Financial effects	Increased turnover >>>	Measurement points: The value of increased customer loyalty
	Reduced costs >>>	Measurement points: The value of the improved resource utilization in the call center
Increased customer satisfaction or resource utilization	Value creation for the call center throgh better resource utilization >>>	Measurement points: Number of dissatisfied customers that leave the organization due to the call center
	Value creation for the CRM department due to increased customer loyalty >>>	Measurement points: Proportion of second calls Average number of calls per agent per hour
Process	Improved ability to handle customer calls >>>	Measurement points: Measure proportion of second calls and calls per agent per hour
Activity	General subject-oriented training >>>	Measurement points: Course evaluations and educational level
	Individual-training and rewards >>>	Measurement points: Employee satisfaction, educational level and rewards

EXHIBIT 3.12   Relationship between Established Measuring Points

resources, but customer loyalty is up. These developments, then, seem to render some positive financial results for the company. But is this actually the case? We think so, but we don't know.

This is why, when using performance management, we are usually not content with just having the measuring points at the time when we need them; we save them, too, for future analyses. For is it actually possible to measure a connection between the general training of call center staff and fewer repeat calls? Or is it solely on the basis of the individual training that we can detect a correlation between training costs and fewer repeat calls? We are therefore very interested in identifying which activity gives the best effect per invested dollar. It is equally valuable to know whether the company via its activities is also achieving its target of reducing call center costs and the number of unhappy customers who cancel their subscriptions. We also want to know how long it will take for the effect to be noticeable. All this we can link to financial goals to analyze which activities render the biggest return.

The objective of performance management is therefore to systematically accumulate experiences based on performed activities by systematically saving and analyzing lag information. This puts us in a position where we can obtain detailed insight into our own processes, an insight that in time means that we can gain a more holistic picture of our organization. What is the correlation between the profiles we employ and how they perform in a call center? Do students perform best? Or do we want to go for the older generation, because we know they'll stay in the job longer? However, are they performing as well as the younger people, if we give them individual training? And do our bonus systems mean that the employee with the biggest bonus stays longer, which would reduce the overall costs of hiring and thereby contribute positively to our HR budgets? All these questions are about striking the right balance. On the one hand, balance is about minimizing the resources used to keeping a process going and, on the other, about ensuring that the process meets the user's expectations.

WHICH PROCESS SHOULD YOU START WITH?

So far in this chapter we have shown how to initiate and optimize operative business processes. In this section, we introduce some specific suggestions for processes that may be suitable for optimization. This section can therefore be read in continuation of the section in Chapter 2 about how to use information as a strategic resource. Whereas Chapter 2 focused on the relationship between corporate strategy and the way information is used, we'll now look at how to optimize operational processes in the individual department of the organization. If we therefore wish to use information as a strategic resource, we can do this in two places from a strategic perspective, as input to the strategy development process, which we covered in Chapter 2, and as a way of creating competitive advantages at the operational level, which is our topic now.

In Chapter 2, we introduced a model that, using three dimensions, shows which disciplines we can compete on. It goes without saying that if an organization has decided on an operational excellence strategy, this will affect the entire business. It is ultimately the operational processes that must ensure that the enterprise can excel in producing and delivering cheaply and effectively and according to customer

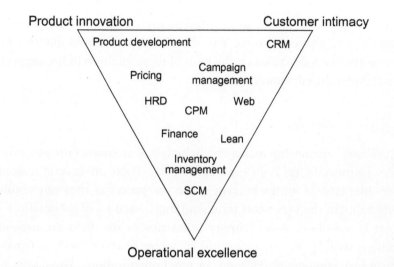

EXHIBIT 3.13 Correlation between Strategy and Operational Processes with Significant Analytical Potential

needs. This leads us to the fact that some analytical disciplines are more relevant to some businesses than to others.

In Chapter 2, we went through how an enterprise can describe its overall competitive parameters via three dimensions. The dimension or dimensions that you found most relevant to your business can be noted in Exhibit 3.13. Thus if you found that your enterprise focuses mostly on customer relations, and not much else, Exhibit 3.13 implies that your analytical focus areas should lie under CRM processes. If you found your enterprise to have its main focus on product innovation, then your analytical focus areas could be to support a number of processes from product development, pricing, campaign management, and CRM, and to integrate these in terms of information.

We have chosen to give eleven suggestions for processes with great analytical potential in the remainder of this chapter. It's debatable whether we should have included fewer or more, and whether the methods we suggest are optimal. This will always be the case in this field. But we have chosen these particular ones because we find that they have proven to be valuable in the past and because we think they will continue to have great value in the future. Similarly, we could discuss their positioning in the triangle. And we will do so for each of the eleven suggestions, without insisting in any way that we are presenting the one and only truth. We refer those who would like to read more about BA described on the basis of these methods to BA-support. com under the education section.

CRM Activities

Customer relationship management activities are one of the processes that historically has been supported by BA. There are several reasons for this. First of all it's because these are processes that can visibly add value in the very short term, and that own a lot of information— that is, customer data. Primary industries in this field are organizations with stable and long-term customer relations, such as banks, insurance companies, telecoms, or relief organizations. The names of individual customers are known and it is possible not only to measure their consumption month by month, but also identify who cancels his or her customer relation. In the following example, we will take our point of departure in the three focus areas of CRM: getting valuable customers, increasing the value of existing customers, and keeping customers.

All in all, this is about optimizing a customer's lifetime value, which equals the average consumption times the number of months this person is a customer, minus costs that are associated with getting this customer. See "the whale" in Exhibit 3.14. Note that the three types of activities—get, increase, and keep—are something companies have always been doing, but when they grow to a certain size, their customers become an undistinguishable mass. Analytical CRM can, so to speak, color customers red, yellow, and blue, and on the basis of these colors, we can carry out individualized initiatives designed to meet the needs of different customer groups.

When we talk about getting valuable customers, we assume two things: that low cost is associated with acquiring the given types of customers and that these customers generate high revenues. A typical analytical technique can therefore be an analysis of which customers have the highest lifetime value: average consumption times average number of months as customers. Next we need to find out through which channels we got the customer, which campaigns

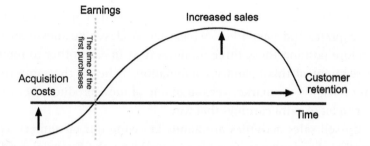

EXHIBIT 3.14 The "Whale" That Shows the Interrelationships between the Three Activities: Get, Increase, and Keep

attracted him or her to penetrate this segment further. This is an analytical method used by telecom companies when they wish to optimize earnings from prepaid subscribers (such as those they get from scratch cards, where the customer's name is not known). In this context, we are interested in learning from which distribution channels the valuable customers buy their scratch cards with a view to focusing sales through this channel.

Another frequently used technique in connection with the optimization of customer lifetime value in the early phase of the relationship is based on new sales via named campaigns. Perhaps we have sent out 1,000 letters or made 1,000 phone calls to get new customers. When the campaign is completed, we can make a profile of the prospects who said yes to our offer. Based on this profile, future activities are focused, on, say, midsized financial institutions, as they seem to be most susceptible to our message. In subsequent campaigns, the message is adapted further to the segment, and advertising resources focus on this target group as this is where the greatest return is to be obtained. This is an analytical method that is essential to sales departments with limited budgets.

If we want to increase our customers' spending, we do so through added sales activities aimed at optimizing customer lifetime value by increasing their average consumption. There are a number of analytical methodologies that support added sales activities. We will look at all of them in the next chapter, which takes its point of departure in analytical methods. A popular method is cross-sales techniques, which look for multiple purchasing patterns. A classic example, which comes from the United Kingdom, describes that men often buy canned beer, frozen pizza, and baked beans together. A clever businessman will therefore position these three products next to each other to remind the segment of this culinary combination. If he, at the same time, chose a slightly up-market version of one of these products, he would secure a bit of extra earnings that way.

Up-sell sales activities are about knowing our customers' consumption development. From banks we know the financial services that follow a customer's life cycle: children's savings account, youth account, family account, pension schemes, and savings plans. Up-sell models are about finding out what to offer the customer next and when, based on his or her last purchase. In addition, these analyses can answer the question of who will typically upgrade to new software versions, or which model of car the customer should be offered next.

Optimization of wallet share is about trying to get the customer to make all his or her purchases in one place (i.e., with us). For example, telecom companies know their corporate customers' consumption. They can then compare this with an estimate of what the customer ought to be consuming based on, for example, Dun & Bradstreet information. Then the number of employees in each of the customer companies is identified, timed with the average consumption per subscriber in the given segment. If we then combine the actual consumption with the estimate of what the customer can be expected to consume, we can identify which customers are likely to be buying from somewhere else, too, and we can then focus on becoming sole supplier—before the competing telecom company does this.

Based on details their customers have given about themselves when receiving their loyalty cards, Tesco, a U.K. supermarket chain, has computed the individual customer's family's "stomach share." This calculation estimates how many calories the customer buys for his or her family in its store. If the number of calories is insufficient to nourish the family, then the store concludes that the customer must be shopping somewhere else, too. Tesco then tries to target more campaigns toward this customer.

When we talk about keeping customers, BA is able, via data mining models, to deliver information about which customers will discontinue their shopping and when. Based on this information, the organization can then come up with some retention products meeting the needs of the individual segments, and thus contact these bargain-hunting customers. BA solutions can also systematically monitor the different ways in which customers are lost: Some customers are happy enough when they leave, but they just had a better offer, while others really are dissatisfied. Sometimes companies themselves reject bad customers. You can read more about this at BA-support.com and in *The Loyalty Effect* by Frederic Reichheld (Harvard Business School Press, 1996). Customer relationship management activities are usually built on value-based segmentation. This makes sense when you think about the 80/20 rule, which says that a business makes 80% of its profit from 20% of its customers. A company will therefore do a lot to retain this 20% and run retention strategies for this group of customers. For example, consider the activities of a large telecom company that let their less valuable customers wait in phone queues, while the best customers were put straight through. The company also made differ-ent retention offers to customers based on their value segment. Some customers were given a free phone along with cinema tickets, while other had to make do with 100 minutes free phone time.

In the middle there is a group of customers that the company will typically try to keep, while at the same time increase their value. Toward this group, added sales techniques are used. Finally, we've got the group of least value. This least valuable 20% usually delivers 1% of the sales. If you then add the fixed costs associated with having these customers, we may well be losing money doing business with them. A business should simply opt out of these customers, or at least minimize all costs when dealing with them.

Campaign Management

This type of analytical process is closely related to CRM activities, but we have moved it a bit toward the operational excellence perspective, because it contains large elements of process optimization in relation to customer dialogue. In more practical terms this means that CRM has to do with making the right campaigns whereas campaign man-agement has an element of optimizing the existing campaigns in terms of automating and developing analytical tools that monitor the cost and performance of the individual campaigns.

We could call these reactive and proactive CRM activities, where the reactive to a great extent is about minimizing problems, such as the retention of customers. This may seem like spending good money on bad customers. It can be necessary, but should rather be looked at as a troubleshooting exercise and a phase the company just has to get through. Proactive CRM activities are more concerned with rewarding and educating good customers and thus investing in loyal customers.

Often loyalty programs will be created that build on an automated dialogue with the customer at the time and with the content that is most valuable to the customer. A customer who is moving can be registered via a change of address in the data warehouse. In such a case, the company could assist with information about the nearest store in the customer's new local community. An alternative, which is used by one of the largest telecom companies, is a continuous update to the customer about which subscription currently delivers the biggest advantages to the customer. In short, these dialogue programs have the aim of making the customer approach our brand and find his or her shoes, rather than customers approaching the shoes and finding our brand.

For this to succeed we need a high degree of automation of our dialogue with customers and analytical competencies to define which customers must have which messages at which times.

In addition, we need to follow up on existing elements in the dialogue program. What gives a positive, negative or no response. And how can we improve our dialogue?

Product Development

This discipline has its obvious place in the product innovation corner of Exhibit 3.13. Innovative processes can be driven by many forces. An example would be strong creative forces, as we know from people in the arts. At other times, processes are initiated by registered customer needs, which are matched with what we expect to be financially optimal. These processes are, as is known from strategy development processes, a combination of art and science, which must form a synthesis, because each of these on its own has a tendency to create only mediocre results.

In this context, BA represents the fact-based element, which sets the scene for the creative processes and the element, which subsequently validates the quality of the creative results via business cases and simulations. We wish to mention, too, data mining in continuation of customer cancellations. For when we have defined which customers typically cancel and described them in a number of dimensions, we are presented with the creative questions: How can we keep customers with a similar profile? And in this way, how can companies continually, and maybe somewhat reactively, adapt their range of services to the needs in the market? The conjoint analysis is another analytical technique, which by means of relatively few customer interviews can deliver information about how many segments we should be developing new products for, and which characteristics each of these products should have, including what the optimum price is.

By deploying this somewhat more proactive route, we can deliver input to the creative process about which attributes the new product must contain, as well as subsequently assess the question about the right price in terms of the costs that are associated with the given proposals.

Web Log Analyses

Web log analyses, and thereby the way in which users click their way around a company's Internet pages, resemble CRM in many ways, as the purpose of the analyses is to understand where our users come from and how to increase their value. We also want to continue to make them use the portal and thereby keep them as customers. The Web log that constitutes the basis for this type of analysis is a file that has one row per click, created on the Web site. This row has information about when the click happened and where the user came from. Often it is possible via cookies or other forms of user ID to recognize and follow the same user over time. Despite its many resemblances with CRM, we have chosen to place this analytical method between customer relations and operational excellence, because Internet portals may have many others purposes, too. These include customer self-service, storage of public information, or as an intranet for staff. If a company has a commercial Internet page, where it sells its products, it must—just as any other store—make the market aware of its existence and its offers. Therefore, we need to perform marketing activities. In continuation of these marketing activities, we would like to understand where our customers came from, what we did right or wrong.

If this is done on the Internet, there are a number of ways of attracting customer attention. We might buy banner ads, which are ads that pop up in other places on the Internet, and where the Internet user is sent to the advertiser's page, if the user clicks on the advertisement. Search engines are another way of attracting attention. The company can search on some key words that the company wants to be associated with and, based on the Internet pages that then appear, decide what to imitate. And we can imitate existing Internet pages to gain a high placing on the results pages of the search engine. A company can make collaborative agreements with other Internet pages, which offer complementary products and mutually refer to each other. Chat rooms and social medias that are used by our customers are other places to attract customer attention and, naturally, we can also choose to run our campaigns via the "old" media.

This also means that in order to know what works and what doesn't, businesses selling their products via Internet stores will be interested in measuring how customers/users are referred to their Web site. Web logs can deliver this information, if users reach the portal via clicking on links, since this will simply be registered in the Web log. From this we can see which marketing activities via Internet referrals deliver good response.

When we are talking about getting customers to increase their usage, it can be helpful to divide them into groups as shown in Exhibit 3.15.

Via the Web log we can see which users are likely to be visiting for the first time and, as we have not registered their identity before, this could be the result of marketing activities. We can see whether the same surfers visit our page several times and, on this background, ensure that they are shown a page that reflects this. They are obviously interested; they have come back, so now we want to try to develop them into what we may call users, which could be achieved by getting

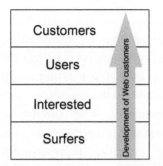

EXHIBIT 3.15 User Types on Our Web Sites

them to create a user profile. On the basis of this user profile, we now know much more about the user and it may well be that he or she subscribes to our newsletter. We will be able to see whether our emails are attention-getting enough for our user to forward them to others in his or her network, who might be interested. Finally, we can develop the user into a customer, which happens when he or she buys from us. Now we know even more about our customer, because we know his or her physical address, which products he or she likes, and we know his or her behavior on our Web site.

From now on we interact with a given customer by running traditional CRM activities to keep and grow him or her. In addition, we have information about which marketing activities result in an actual sale. We can now follow the entire development, from banner advertisement to purchase, and learn from this. Are there any geographical areas that we should advertise more in? Are there places on the Internet, where we should advertise more, etc.? How did the customer develop over time, and which pages did he or she look at prior to purchasing? How many times do people visit our Web site before they make their first purchase, and how can we improve this process?

When we talk about retaining customers, it's largely the same analytical methods that are used as in conventional CRM. However, the key issue here may be "when did we lose a given customer?". Is it when he or she canceled his or her newsletter, or when there has been no purchase in a year, or when the customer moves down into a lower value segment, or perhaps something else?

At the time of writing, we are amazed at how few resources are actually used to analyze Web log information. It's true that the dot com time is dot gone, as the saying goes, but the vision behind the dot com trend is as real as ever. The Internet is still a parallel universe to the physical distribution, with enormous potential, both independently and in combination with the physical distribution. And the large shift did happen; consumers have gotten used to using the Internet. So the big revolution represented by the dot com trend has been more of a trickling process, with businesses waiting for people to start shopping on the Internet. Now the consumers are about to be ready and, ironically, we now seem to be waiting for stores to get ready.

Pricing

We have chosen to place pricing in the product innovation corner, because we feel that price is an essential element of a product. Versace and Rolex would, for instance, not be the same, if they could be purchased for $20 in the nearest supermarket.

Pricing is a subject in its own right in the field of marketing. Price is hugely connected with the position the company's brand has or wishes to have in the market. We can work with this analytically, too, but analytical optimization is first and foremost about identifying which price a given product with its given characteristics, for a given segment, should have. The product may be new, so we have little or no historical information to work with, and we therefore want to use a conjoint analysis as mentioned in the previous section on product development. Alternatively, the product (or a similar product) may have been on the market a number of years, and we therefore have a lot of historical information to work with.

The techniques used in this context are called forecasting techniques. These techniques consist of two phases. The first is about understanding the correlation and, based on this, developing a model. The next phase is about using the model to find the optimum mix of price, amount, and marketing activities. Questions to be answered in the first phase could be:

- How big an impact do my competitors' prices have on my revenues?
- If I carry out a campaign, how big an effect will it have on sales?
- When will I see the effect of the campaign and when will it stop?
- How do I adjust my activities in connection with seasonal, weekly, or daily variations?
- What are the synergies between advertisements in different media?
- What will my sales be in the coming quarters?

When you get to phase two, you'll have knowledge about the market mechanisms under which you operate, which means that you are in a position to adjust your business behavior. Specifically, this can be done via simulations such as these: What happens if I employ another salesperson, if I increase or reduce my price, or carry out more and/or combined campaigns? You will, in other words, be in possession of analytical input to support the optimization of the company's marketing mix. It all sounds rather complex, but the market offers software that makes it surprisingly easy and cheap to deliver these correlations.

Human Resource Development

In the middle of Exhibit 3.13, we have placed human resource development (HRD), which consists of processes, excluding the purely administrative, that spring from the human resources function. The reason is that the three competitive disciplines that are described by the model are never going to be any better than the people who perform them. It is the qualified and motivated employees who are often the scarcest resource in modern organizations. In this context, it's a wonder that more major organizations, including wholly or partly public institutions, don't employ analytical HRD. We are talking about very large volumes of data that describe employees based on dimensions such as illness, education, target achievement, gender, age, manager, department, career route. So the data material is already there.

The biggest hurdle here may be the culture that exists in HR departments, with its strong focus on creativity and soft values. Thus, it can seem provocative to present analytical facts, however qualified. We therefore have to approach this professional area via strong sponsors high up in the organization, since a noncommitted culture, as we know, can eat any strategy for breakfast.

If we look at analytical CRM, the approach from this field can be used in connection with analytical HRD, because we need to be able to attract the right employees, optimize their performance, and retain the best—that is, get, increase, keep. The objective is therefore comparable with the one we know from CRM. The means are, however, completely different, because in HR we can develop employees via new hiring and talks with existing staff, with focus on satisfaction surveys, professional or personal development, and/or reward systems.

In terms of attracting the right employees, we can take future desired states into consideration via analyses of which groups of employees perform above average.

When we are talking about optimizing performance, this could happen by associating the motivation of individual employees with their absence due to illness. Employees in the municipalities of Copenhagen and Aarhus in Denmark have, for instance, accrued more than 20 days of absence due to illness per year, whereas employees in bordering local municipalities have accrued less than half that. The profiling of which groups of employees have a lot of absence due to illness can therefore provide a good basis for targeted initiatives adapted to the individual employee's need for motivation. To quote from another context: "If our employees are the organization's most important resource, then it is management's most important mission to ensure they turn up for work again tomorrow."

Employee retention is also a discipline that can render huge value creation. Losing and hiring a typical professional leads to costs of around $50,000. So what must the company offer its employees to ensure that they are still there same time, next year? Is it possible to offer employees a month or two of working only 80% of a 40-hour week, with a corresponding salary reduction, while their house is being renovated? Is it possible, with no change in salary, to offer employees a company car, share options, or professional or personal development?

Questions such as these can be answered via analyses of question-naire data and interviews with employees, who are leaving the company. The company can, with good reason, view its employees as customers who pay with their work. And as a thank-you for their work, employees should receive individualized counter services, which is a mix of salary, leisure time, personal and professional development, etc. For more about this subject in connection with the presentation of the SIPOC model, see Chapter 8.

CPM

We will only mention this subject briefly here, as it is covered in the section on optimizing existing business processes earlier in this chapter. Corporate performance management is about measuring processes (performance management) in order to understand the correlation between process-improving activities and their effect, with a view to further improving the processes. We have chosen to place CPM in the middle of the triangle to indicate that the desired learning may relate to innovation, customer relationships, and operational excellence.

If we focus solely on the Six Sigma and the Lean approaches, focus will move toward the operational excellence corner, depending on to the extent you want to include the customer's needs when establishing new processes. Through so-called control charts, we also get some useful alternative tools to monitor our processes, and they will tell us whether we have managed to influence them positively via our process-improving initiatives.

Finance

Activity-based costing (ABC) is about being able to allocate the company's costs to the processes that are generating them. The purpose of this is to enable us to subsequently assess which products or customer groups are profitable. Generally speaking, it therefore gives the company a clearer idea of where its significant costs are. If some processes represent great costs, and these processes are not essential to the company's competitive situation, outsourcing of these should be considered. If, for instance, a company produces designer goods and has a significant profit margin on this, but at the same time is running a number of shops with a small profit margin, this could obviously prompt considerations as to whether it might be an idea to sell the shops and focus resources on the most successful area. Similar considerations may have resulted in Shell Denmark selling all its shops to 7-Eleven in 2007. Shell is good at creating high-profit margins in the energy industry, but less so in retail. And vice versa with 7-Eleven.

If we combine ABC, which is about knowing our cost structure, with conjoint analyses or other pricing methods, which are about sales potential, we get some strong tools, which enable the company to optimize based on profit margin.

Lean is another approach to minimizing costs. Here we constantly work toward what has been defined as an optimum process. Whatever is between the actual process and the optimum one is described as a waste of resources and the cost should be cut. Critics of this method maintain that this is about process optimization, but not necessarily well-being, which is why Lean measurements benefit from being supplemented by employee satisfaction surveys (analytical HRD) to give the full picture.

Inventory Management

We are now far down in the operational excellence corner of Exhibit 3.13, where our optimizations can be difficult to link to direct customer relations, and the future product development. This applies to inventory management, too, as this is concerned with ensuring that the people who draw on the inventory must always be able to get what they want. If they can't, production will grind to a halt, whether it's the spare part or raw material inventory that has gone into back order. If the product inventory is empty, customers will be waiting. Being overstocked, on the other hand, represents an unfortunate situation of tied-up capital, and the risk of stocked items becoming outdated and losing value.

An analytical approach delivers decision support to the people responsible for inventory management in terms of identifying the optimum number of items in stock. Of course, there's always the risk of the occasional empty shelf, but that is a calculated risk. Any loss that is incurred because of empty shelves is compensated for by less tied-up capital by means of overall smaller stock. As described in connection with CPM, analytical tools deliver the possibility of a continuous monitoring of which stock items are unavailable too often and enable the company to continuously adapt its inventory.

Supply Chain Management

Supply chain management (SCM) is about managing the company's relations to its suppliers. These relations vary from company to company and from supplier to supplier. At one end of the spectrum, we've got strategic collaborations where the companies' processes become as one, and we're working with joint development projects of products and logistics. At the other end, we find relations characterized by sporadic relations, where alternative suppliers can always be found. In terms of strategic collaborations, the analytical methods will reflect the same methods that are used for internal optimizations. These could be ABC, Lean, or CPM, as shown earlier.

With regard to the more casual supplier relations, where price is negotiated from deal to deal, the required information will be more about giving the buying organization complete details about its suppliers. This can be seen as a countermove to the CRM information held by the selling organization and that is used to optimize its sales processes.

It may sound trivial, but this ultimately has to do with the fact that large companies, such as A.P. Moeller (APM) which is a conglomerate within the energy and shipping industry, have thousands of suppliers worldwide, and these suppliers are specialists in their fields. A.P. Moeller is therefore in a weaker negotiating position than the seller. The countermove here is to ensure that the buying organization has information about how to get the same service from somewhere else. It would work to strengthen APM's bargaining position, too, to know whether the company is a major buyer of services from the individual supplier, making the company a key customer that the supplier wouldn't lose for anything. For the relatively large company, analytical SCM is about obtaining all the details about the many suppliers, so that the company has in-depth knowledge about the pricing in the supplier market, with the result that it could exploit a strategic customer position.

Lean

It could be argued that Lean should be placed in the middle of the Exhibit 3.13 since you also can lean your product development processes and since when you buy a service you are essentially a process based on your needs. However we placed it in the right side of Exhibit 3.13 because Lean essentially is the discipline of balancing internal resource utilization with what the customers' wants.

There are many ways to optimize processes essentially however; they all have the same purpose of optimizing the balance between how you as a company deploy your costs and what makes the customers of the process satisfied. There is no universal balance that it in itself is the optimal. It depends on your organizational strategy and customer expectations. For example, at both the Waldorf and Burger King you can get a meal; however, these are very different experiences. This also means that when you design the way customers must queue in a Burger King restaurant they are quite unlikely to get any free champagne as opposed to what they might receive at the Waldorf.

There are several terms used for this way of improving your business model such as *business process reengineering, Lean, Six Sigma, operational excellence* or *process excellence*. The essence of this approach is that the changes that you set out to do, via the different tool boxes, is specifically approached from a process perspective as opposed to other disciplines which are more departmentally focused (e.g., procurement, inventory, finance, marketing, etc.).

In brief, analytics primarily support this way of making organizational improvements in three ways. First, learn what the customers want before you start changing the process: This can be done through surveys that ask customers about the basics that the Waldorf has to get right when you are queuing, like indoor seating and a good social atmosphere. Find out what the customers are willing to pay. Finally, find out what would delight the customers and could be a business differentiator, which could be the champagne mentioned before. As a starting point, however, analytics could also text mine customer comments in order to get an idea about what should be included in the questionnaire in the first place. As a general rule text mining in the form of complaints will give you an indication of what basics that you do wrong occasionally, whereas the more you get toward the delight factors such as champagne in the queue, the more you have to rely on creative and non-data driven sessions.

To learn whether the customers actually like the new process that you have envisioned, questionnaire information can help process owners to see how it affects customer satisfaction. The critical question is whether the company has achieved the right balance between how they spend their resources and what is rewarded by an increased willingness to pay a higher price by the customers. Alternatively, some organizations seek the right balance between how they spend their resources and the change in customer loyalty under the assumption that a mathematical relationship between the customer loyalty and what the customers spend has been established. The critical questions could be: Have we made the process so cheaply designed that it does not live up to our customer's expectations set? Are we spending money on something that the customers don't really value anyway?

To learn about the processes on a continuous basis, analytics also monitor existing processes for changes via control charts that indicate whether the process performance has changed significantly from a statistical perspective. This can answer questions like: Has the process improved? Has it become more stable and predictable? Companies with a great focus on Lean will often have a process owner who in turn has a control chart of the particular process which is revisited every day. The purpose of a control chart is to see whether there are any changes in the performance of the processes or alternatively how the company can benefit from or minimize the damage of the change. Text mining through a customer satisfaction survey could also be relevant for process owners since a control chart only sends a signal telling that something is wrong. However, written input from customers might give you input about what causes problems from a customer perspective.

A CATALOGUE OF IDEAS WITH KPIs FOR THE COMPANY'S DIFFERENT FUNCTIONS

Exhibit 3.16 lists KPIs. This is not a complete list, nor do we intend for it to be indicative of which KPIs are more correct than others. Its aim is to provide you with inspiration. As always, KPIs are measuring points linking activities to objectives. KPIs help to maintain the organization's focus on its objectives by appointing people who are responsible for their attainment. In addition, KPIs give the organization the opportunity to learn about its own processes.

EXHIBIT 3.16 Catalogue of Ideas with KPIs for the Company's Different Functions

Function	KPI
Executive Management	ROE—Return on equity
	Share price
Sales and Marketing	Sales to new customers
	Growth in sales
	Number of new customers
	Number of customer meetings
	Number of new orders
	Average earning per customer
	Change in customer lifetime value
	Customer discounts
	Average price
	Pipeline/sales ratio
	Market share
	Market growth rate
	Number of new campaigns
	Competitors' growth
	Competitors' market share
Human Resources	Average years of employment
	Employee revenue
	Number of employees/Budgeted headcount
	Results of employee satisfaction surveys
	Number of open positions
	Voluntary and involuntary employee reduction
	New positions filled by women/men
	Number of run-down employees/stress

Function	KPI
Production	Operational errors
	Process costs
	Number of faulty units
	Number of deliveries on time
	Inventory
	Number of inventory days
	Capacity utilization
	Purchasing prices
	Number of completed process improvement initiatives via Kaizen methodology
IT and Development	Systems uptime
	Number of deliveries on time
	Operational loss due to breakdown
	Time from event to solution
Customer Service	Number complaints
	Incorrect deliveries
	Returned units
	Average processing time
Finance	Number of completed process improvement initiatives via Kaizen methodology
	Individual targets
	Delivery of accounts and reports on time
	Number of requests from the business for clarification

SUMMARY

In this chapter, we explained the difference between lead and lag information as well as their role in connection with the establishing of processes.

Lag information is retrospective information, which we choose to register on an ongoing basis in our data warehouse in connection with performance management.

Lead information has a completely different character than lag information. Lead information is used to improve business processes or initiate new business processes. Lead information in the BA framework is typically created on the basis of an analysis of lag information and is therefore usually not stored in tables, since this information, as already mentioned, is the outcome of an analytical process. Lead information will typically have the character of "breaking insight," which can be used to improve overall business processes, and provide learning loops back to the strategic level.

Then we looked at how we can identify critical information in connection with the establishing of new business processes based on a Rockart model. The BA function will often be working with the optimization of existing processes, too, and we showed how to do this based on CPM and our own models.

Finally, we described eleven operational professional areas and processes where BA information can make a positive difference. The methods were related to the three competitive parameters from Chapter 2, in which we introduced information as a strategic resource in a strategic context.

CHAPTER 4

Business Analytics at the Analytical Level

This chapter describes the third level in the business analytics (BA) model that constitutes the underlying principle of this book. Chapters 1 and 2 explained the kinds of information an organization typically asks for at a strategic level, and which requirements for information this leads to at the department level.

In this chapter, we'll be taking a closer look at the different analytical methods that generate and deliver the required information and knowledge. We will not be discussing the technical aspects of a delivery, as this will be included in Chapter 5 about the data warehouse, but we will focus entirely on which methods can generate which types of decision support for the business.

The purpose of this chapter is to create a basis for dialogue between the company and the analyst. The chapter represents a menu that provides the company with an overview of which types of information and knowledge they can ask for and equally provides the analyst with an understanding of how the dish (the analytical method) is prepared and from which ingredients (data). To support this process, we have included an outline for a specification of requirements, so that you can gain an overview of which issues need to be covered in the dialogue.

The size of the menu is always debatable; the chef thinks he or she offers plenty of choice, while customers want to see as many dishes as possible. We have chosen a menu size that corresponds to what anyone can reasonably expect an analyst to master methodwise, or what an analyst would be able to learn during two to three weeks of training. Generally speaking, however, we assume that Microsoft Excel in its present form (2010) is just a spreadsheet (which is even capable of providing basic statistics), and that a quantitative analyst needs a statistical program. In the current market, it is our opinion that the leading analytical software vendors are SAS and SPSS. Note, too, that both software vendors offer short courses in the analytical methods that are introduced in this chapter.

This chapter breaks down different types of knowledge and information in a way that makes it possible for the company to formulate exactly what it wants from its BA function. Furthermore, we are listing the different analytical methods that can produce the required input to the company—that is, we are translating information requirements into "analyst language." Note that, as a reader of this book, you have access to the Web site BA-support.com, which consists of a large number of statistical examples and an interactive statistics book. Both can guide you, as an analyst, in your search for which methods to use under which circumstances.

The focus in this chapter is not on method or statistics, but rather on demonstrating the connection between the BA function and the deliveries of information and knowledge that the BA function must subsequently produce. The business wants information and knowledge, while analysts conduct data mining and provide both statistics and tables based on data.

DATA, INFORMATION, AND KNOWLEDGE

In this book, we distinguish between the three concepts: data, information, and knowledge. This chapter in particular emphasizes this distinction, which is why we'll go through the terms briefly. *Data* is defined as the carrier of information. Data, as such, seldom delivers, line by line, fact by fact, or category by category any value to the user. An example of a piece of data could be "bread" or "10.95." Data is often too specific to be useful to us as decision support. It is a bit like reading through a data warehouse from A to Z, and then expecting to be able to answer every question. We are deep down at a detailed level, where we simply can't see the wood for the trees. Besides, data in a data warehouse is not structured in any single way that makes sense; rather, it could potentially make sense in many contexts.

Information is data that is aggregated to a level where it makes sense for decision support in the shape of, for instance, reports, tables, or lists. An example of information could be that the sales of bread in the last three months have been respectively $18,000, $23,000, and $19,000. We can generate this information in the BA department and then deliver it to the person who is responsible for bread sales, and this person could then analyze this information, draw conclusions, and initiate the actions that are deemed relevant. When our deliveries consist of information, we are able to automate the process. This requires initial resources, but it requires those resources only once. It doesn't take a lot of analyst resources thereafter. When we say that the BA department generates *knowledge*, this doesn't mean that it generates just information to the user, but that this information has been analyzed and interpreted. This means that the BA department, as an example, offers some suggestions regarding why bread sales have fluctuated in the last three months. Reasons could be seasonal fluctuations, campaigns, new distributions conditions, or competitors' initiatives. It is therefore not a question of handing the user a table, but instead of supplementing this table with a report or a presentation. This means, of course, that when the BA department delivers knowledge, it is not a result of an automated process, as in connection with report generation, but rather a process that requires analysts with quantitative methods and business insight.

ANALYST'S ROLE IN THE BA MODEL

Of course, organizations vary, but generally speaking there are certain requirements that we expect analysts to meet, and therefore certain competencies that must be represented if we want a smoothly running

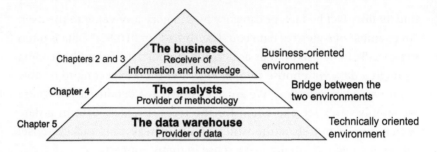

EXHIBIT 4.1   The Analyst's Role in the Business Analysis Model

analytics function. We'll take a closer look at the implication of whether these competencies are covered by each individual analyst or whether these competencies are covered jointly across the analytics team or the rest of the organization. But what is important is that the competencies are present, since without them the BA function will not be able to link the technical side of the organization to the business side. We're talking about linking two completely different perspectives as illustrated in Exhibit 4.1. Technicians have a tendency to perceive the organization as a large number of technologies that together constitute a systems structure, in relation to which data from the source systems moves. This perspective is incompatible with a business perspective, which sees the organization as a large number of value-adding processes that ultimately deliver different types of services or products to its customers.

The danger of assuming the technically oriented perspective is that operating and maintaining the company's technical systems' structure might end up being an objective in itself. The consequence is what is called "a data warehouse with a life of its own," independent of the rest of the organization's need for information. Symptoms include huge volumes of data of such poor quality or lack of relevance that they are useless to the organization. Such a situation means that the investment made by the organization is in fact merely a cost, as nothing valuable comes of it. Other symptoms might be that every time you want to enter new information in your data warehouse you just can't, because the technical side is working on a project that the business has not asked for. The system is thus using all its resources on self-maintenance and has none left for serving the business. Again, we've got an investment that is yielding no return.

At an operational level, symptoms include the delivery of front-ends that are not user-friendly. The front-ends might show the required information, but not in a way that is practical from a user point of view, because they forgot to ask the users what they wanted. If these symptoms are noted, we often find a general reluctance to use data warehouse information, too. It follows then that the business does not take the time to enter data in a thorough way, for example when salespeople have met with customers. The result is a further fragmentation of data and consequently a reluctance to use the data warehouse. Over time, an internal decision structure emerges that is not based on data warehouse information, unless it is strictly necessary, and the entire argument for creating a data warehouse then disappears. When the decision was made to invest in a data warehouse the purpose was to improve the general decision behavior, which is the value-adding element of a data warehouse. So, again, we see an investment that is yielding no return.

All this can happen when the company does not have an information strategy that clearly uses the data warehouse as a means of attaining business objectives. So, first and foremost, we need to ensure we've got a process, an *information strategy*, that ensures the coordination between the business and the data warehouse. But at the same time we need to make some demands on the analyst's tool kit (i.e., we make some requirements regarding specific analytical competencies that are present in the company). The old rule applies here that a chain is only as strong as its weakest link. A company might possess perfect data material on the one hand and some clearly formulated requirements for information on the other, but the overall result will be only as good as the analysts are able to make it. Some companies invest millions a year in their data warehouse and yet hire analysts who are really only data managers or report developers, which means that they are unable to contribute with any independent analytical input, but can merely deliver reports, tables, or lists within a few days. The company therefore spends millions a year on technology and its maintenance and receives only a few reports, tables, and lists, because it never invested sufficiently in the people side of an information system.

THREE REQUIREMENTS THE ANALYST MUST MEET

Based on these premises, we can specify three clear requirements of our analysts, their competency center, or their performance of individual tasks:

- Business competencies
- Tool kit must be in order (method competencies)
- Technical understanding (data competencies)

Business Competencies

First of all, the analyst must understand the business process he or she is supporting and how the delivered information or the delivered knowledge can make a value-adding difference at a strategic level. In this context, when we talk about a strategic level, it is implied, too, that we need analytical competencies: the analyst understands and is able to convey to the business the potential of using the information as a competitive parameter. This is essential if the BA function is to participate independently and proactively in value creation, and it is likewise essential that we can therefore talk about information as a strategic asset. The analyst needs to have or be given a fundamental business insight in relation to the deliveries that are to be made. This insight is necessary so that the analyst stands a chance of maximizing his or her value creation. The analyst must also be able to independently optimize the information or the knowledge in such a way that the user is given the best possible decision support. This also enables analysts to approach individual business process owners on an ongoing basis and present them with knowledge that is generated in connection with other contexts. The analyst needs to be capable of having a continual dialogue with the business, as well as be capable of detecting and creating synergies across functions.

Analysts must be able to see themselves in the bigger context as illustrated in the following story about the traveler and the two stonemasons. The traveler met one stonemason, asked him what he was doing, and got the reply that he was cutting stones, that each had to be 15 by 15 by 15, and that he had to deliver 300 stones a day. Later on, the traveler came across another stonemason and asked the same question, but here got the reply: "I am building the largest and most beautiful cathedral in all of the country, and through this cathedral, good tidings will be spread throughout the land." In other words, analysts must be able to see their function in the broader picture, so they are not only performing a number of tasks, but are able to get the biggest possible value from the volume of information and knowledge they obtain and develop every single day.

Tool Kit Must Be in Order (Method Competencies)

An analyst's answer, regardless of the question, should never be simply, "I'll give you a table." Of course, a table can be the right solution at times, but tables can be enormous. It is therefore a reasonable requirement that the analyst is able to make suggestions about whether statistical testing is needed to show any correlations that might be present in the tables. The analyst might also be able to visualize the information in such a way that the user gets an overview of all the data material in the first place.

Moreover, the analyst must be able to deliver more than information in a model and take part in the analysis of this information to ensure that the relevant knowledge is obtained. There is another important aspect in the analyst's role in securing that the users of the information derive the right knowledge from it. We cannot even begin to count the times we've been sitting at a presentation with bar charts of different heights, where people go for the "red" segment, because it has the highest average score. In this context, it could be pointed out that it would have been extraordinary if the averages had been exactly the same. This brings up the question about how different the averages must be before we're allowed to conclude that there is a difference and therefore a basis for a new segment and new business initiatives. The problem is that the decision has not been subjected to quality-assurance validation via a simple statistical test. Such a test could prompt us to ask if we make a decision based on these figures, are we then likely to draw the wrong conclusion? Note here that we are not proposing that a requirement for the analyst be that he or she must be able to explain covariance matrices. That's not that important these days, when we have software for all the calculations. But the requirement for the analyst is that he or she have a basic knowledge of which test to use when and be able to draw the right conclusions from the test. As mentioned earlier in this chapter, this is knowledge that is communicated via two- to five-day training courses that have been run by leading suppliers of analytical software (not traditional business intelligence software).

Another problem that we often encounter among analysts is that they are reluctant to work with software that is new to them. This means that they have a tendency to define themselves as software programmers rather than as analysts. The bottom line is that we have approximately three to four vendors of relevant analytical software, offering 10 to 12 software packages, and the key to finding the optimum combination is a continual search-and-learn process. It is not about what the individual analyst has by now become familiar with and is comfortable programming and clicking around in. It is worth pointing out that most analytical software packages across vendors work well together. If a company has a software package that does not integrate well with other software, the company should consider replacing it, because it can limit the analysts' capabilities. All software packages differ enormously on dimensions such as price, user-friendliness (crucial to how fast an analysis can be performed), integration with data sources, the ability to solve specific problems, guarantees of future updates, ability to automate reports, technical support, analytical support, and training courses. If in doubt, start by taking a course in any given software, and then decide whether you want to buy it.

Technical Understanding (Data Competencies)

The final requirement that we must make of analysts is that they have a basic understanding of how to retrieve and process data. Again, this is about how to structure processes, because just as analysts have to sometimes draw on support from the business in connection with the creation of information and knowledge, they must also be able to draw directly on data warehouse competencies. If, for instance, an analyst needs new data in connection with a task, it's no good if he or she needs several days to figure out how the Structured Query Language (SQL) works, what the different categories mean, or whether value-added tax is included in the figures. We therefore need the data warehouse to have a support function where people understand their role in the BA value chain. However, analysts spend about 80% of their time retrieving and presenting data, so we also have to place some clear demands on the analysts' competencies in connection with data processing.

In conclusion, analysts need to master three professional competencies to be successful: business, method, and data. We can add to this certain key personal competencies: the ability to listen and to convince. These are necessary if a task is to be understood, discussed with all involved parties, and delivered in such a way that it makes a difference to business processes and thereby becomes potentially value-adding.

All in all, it sounds as if we need a superman. And that might not be far off, considering the fact that this is the analytical age. And, if we recognize information as a potential strategic asset, then this is another area in which we need to invest, both in the public education sector and in individual companies. Note, however, that these personal and professional skills do not need to be encompassed in a single person; they just need to be represented in the organization and linked when required. We will discuss this in more detail in Chapter 7, where we discuss BA in an organizational context.

REQUIRED COMPETENCIES FOR THE ANALYST

An analyst derives only a fraction of the knowledge that is potential if he fails to use the correct analytical methodology. Analysts can therefore generate considerable loss in value, if they are the weak link in the process.

Analytical Methods (Information Domains)

In the previous section, we discussed the analyst's role in the overall BA value chain, which stretches from collecting data in the technical part of the organization to delivering information or knowledge to the business-oriented part of the organization. We outlined some requirements of the analytical function, one of which was that it must function as a bridge between the technical side and the business side of the organization, and thereby form a value chain or a value-creating process.

Another requirement is that the analytical function must possess methodical competencies to prevent loss of information. Loss of information occurs when the accessible data in a data warehouse, provided it is retrieved and analyzed in an optimum way, has the potential of delivering business support of a certain quality, but cannot because this quality is compromised. Reasons for this lack might be the simple failure to collect the right information, which might, in turn, be due to lack of knowledge about the data or lack of understanding of how to retrieve it.

But errors might also be traced to the analyst not having the necessary tool kit in terms of methodology. When this is the case, the analyst derives only a fraction of the knowledge that is potentially there. If we therefore imagine that we have a number of analysts who are able to extract only 50% of the potential knowledge in the data warehouse in terms of business requirements, we have a corresponding loss from our data warehouse investment. When we made the decision to invest in a data warehouse based on our business case, we naturally assumed that we would obtain something close to the maximum knowledge. Instead, we end up getting only half the return on our investment. That means that the data warehouse investment in the business case should have been twice as big. If we look at the business case from this perspective, it might not have been a profitable decision to acquire a data warehouse, which means the investment should not have been made. Analysts can therefore generate considerable loss in value, if they are the weak link in the process.

Therefore, in the following section we have prepared a list of methods that provide the BA department with a general knowledge of the methodological spectrum as well as a guide to finding your way around it.

How to Select the Analytical Method

In Chapter 3, we performed a so-called *strategy mapping* process (i.e., we presented a method where we had some strategic objectives and ended up with having some specific information requirements). Now, we will pick up this thread. We will perform an *information mapping* process, where we start with some specific information requirements and proceed to identify which specific analytical techniques will deliver the required knowledge or the desired information.

The aim is to present a model that can be used in the dialogue between management who wants information and the analyst who must deliver it. In the introduction to this chapter, we said that we would be delivering a *menu*. What we want to deliver here, too, are some key questions to ensure that the dialogue between analyst and recipient provides an overview of how this menu is designed to facilitate the right information being ordered. More specifically, this means that we divide potential BA deliveries into four information types (see Exhibit 4.2), deliver the questions that will help clarify which information types are the most relevant, and go through the four information types one by one. Concentrate on the type that is relevant to you.

In terms of perspective, we start with a business perspective and finish with an analytical perspective. We begin, for example, with requesting information about which customers will be leaving us in the next month, and finish, perhaps, with the answer that a neural network will be a good candidate in terms of selecting a method of delivering results. The business-oriented reader who wants to understand more about scalability levels, say, can log on to BA-support.com, where we have included an interactive statistics book, along with a number of examples and case studies. Finally, you will find contact details for the authors of this book.

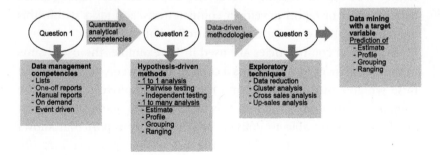

EXHIBIT 4.2 The Three Imperatives in Connection with Choice of Methods and Information Mapping

The Three Imperatives

We obviously are not suggesting that the analyst read through this whole text every time he or she needs to determine which methods to use to deliver which information or which knowledge. The idea is that the analyst has read the text beforehand, and is able to implicitly draw from it in his or her dialogue with the business. The following three points can be useful in selecting the relevant method.

Question 1: Determine with the process owner whether the quantitative analytical competencies, or the data manager and report developer competencies are required. Analytical competencies here mean knowledge about statistical, exploratory data mining, and operations research competencies with the objective of generating knowledge and information. Data manager or report developer competencies refer to the ability to retrieve and present the right information in list or table form. Data manager or report developer competencies are therefore about retrieving and presenting the right information in the right way, without any kind of interpretation of this information via analytical techniques. One scenario might be that a number of graphs are generated in connection with delivery, providing a visualized overview of the information in the table, but without any test to help the user prioritize this information. In other words, data managers or report developers deliver information and leave its interpretation to its users. Of course, there are examples of data managers or report developers who produce tables or reports, and then prepare a business case based on this information. However, this does not make them quantitative analysts. Rather, it's a case of wearing several hats. So, we are here talking about data manager or report developer competencies, and tasks within this domain are solved by wearing the controller hat, so to speak.

Analytical competencies are used if, for example, the user wants to find the answer to, "Is there is a correlation between how much of a raise we give our employees and the risk of employees leaving the company within one year?" In this case, the data manager or report developer will be able to deliver only a table or report that shows employees in groups according to the size of their pay increase, and what percentage within each group have changed jobs. The analyst (with a statistical solution) will be able to say, "Yes, we can say with

99% certainty that there is a correlation." The analyst is therefore not only creating information, but knowledge, too.

If the user wanted answers to questions like, "Do any of our customers have needs that resemble each other? If so, what are those needs?" then the data manager or report developer would be faced with a big challenge. He or she must now prepare reports and tables showing everyone who bought product A as well as which other products they purchased, too. There is a similar reporting need for products B, C, and through the last product. Detecting correlations can become a large and complex puzzle. And the interpretation therefore depends on the eye of the beholder. The analyst (explorative analytics) will, via cluster models, identify different customer groups that have comparable consumption patterns and then segment the customer base, based on the identified clusters.

If the user wanted an answer to a question like, "Which customers are going to leave us next month and why?," the data manager or report developer would deliver a large number of tables or reports that, based on information that is available about customers, can deliver a percentage figure of how many customers stayed and how many discontinued their customer relations. The analyst (data mining analytics with target variables) will be able to deliver models describing the different customer segments who often discontinue their customer relations as well as pinpointing which specific customers must be expected to leave the company next month.

Question 2: Determine whether hypothesis-driven analytics, or data-driven analytics can be expected to render the best decision support. What we call hypothesis-driven analytics could also be called the statistical method domain (note that descriptive statistics such as summations, means, minimum, maximum, or standard deviations are within the data manager domain), and its primary purpose is to create knowledge about correlations between different factors, such as age and purchasing tendencies or pay increase and job loyalty.

One of the problems in using traditional statistical tests is that 1 in 20 times a correlation will be found that does not actually exist. This is because we are working with a confidence level of 5%, which in turn means that if we are 95% certain, we conclude that there is a correlation. In 1 in 20 tests between variables that have nothing to do with each other, we will therefore find a statistical correlation anyway corresponding to the 5%. To minimize this phenomenon, a general rule is applied that says that to ensure the quality of the conclusions they must have theoretical relevance. Note here that those tests are performed only when we have a test sample and want to show some general correlations in the population it describes. If you have the entire population, there is no reason to test whether men are earning more than women. That is obviously just a question of looking at the average figures in a standard report.

Data-driven methods also have the purpose of creating knowledge about some general correlations, but are focused more strongly on creating models for specific decision support at the customer or subscriber level. The big difference between data mining and explorative analytics on the one hand, and hypothesis statistics on the other lies in how we conduct quality assurance testing on our results. Data mining is not theoretically driven like statistics. Data mining is data driven. This means that data mining analysts will typically let the algorithms find the optimum model, without any major theoretical restrictions. And the quality of the model then depends on how performs on a data set set aside for this validation process.

To a certain extent, however, there is an overlap between some models, since we can conduct quality assurance on results by asking for theoretical significance, before even bothering to test the correlations. Similarly, we can develop models via the same method as a data-driven process, and then subsequently test whether the correlations shown by the models can be generalized in a broader sense by examining how successful they are in making predictions on other datasets than on the ones they have been developed on.

As explained earlier, the big difference between hypothesis analytics and data-driven analytics is how quality assurance testing is conducted on their results. But how do we know which route to take to reach our target? In the following section, we'll list a number of things to be aware of when choosing which route to take. Note here that it isn't important whether we choose one method or the other. Rather, the important thing is to generate the right information or the right knowledge for the company's subsequent decision making. Generally speaking, the target is the main thing, although we're here looking at the means.

If the aim is to generate knowledge to be used in a purely scientific context, the answer is unambiguously to adopt the hypothesis-driven approach. It's not really a question of what gives the *best* results, but rather it's a question of completing the formalities to ensure that others with the same data and the same method can get the same results and can relate critically to these. This is possible when using statistical analytics, but not when using data mining analytics because they are based on sampling techniques. We will look at these in the section on data mining. If colleagues are to be able to re-create the results in connection with the validation of generated knowledge at higher levels in the organization, the arguments for the hypothesis-driven approach are very strong.

Hypothesis-driven analytics are to be preferred if we just want to describe correlations of data in pairs. It is just a question of getting an answer to whether the correlations we find can be ascribed to coincidences in our test sample or whether we can assume that they vary as described in our theory. Typical questions here could be "Did a campaign have any effect? Yes or no?" "Do men spend more than women?" "Are sales bigger per salesperson in one state than in another?"

Data-driven analytics are typically preferred for tasks that are complex for different reasons, where customer information is an example of data that constantly changes, large amounts of data and limited initial knowledge about correlations in the data material. This often creates a situation where analysts within a company are drowning in data, while the rest of the organization is thirsting for information and knowledge since the analysts speed of analysis' simply cannot keep up with need for knowledge based on ever-changing near–real time data. Business environments increasingly find themselves in this situation, where enormous amounts of customer information are accumulated, but they are finding it difficult to unlock this information in a way that adds value.

A classic example could be a campaign, which has been prepared and sent to all customers. Some customers have accepted the offer, and others haven't. The questions now are "What can we learn from the campaign, and how can we make sure that the next campaign offers something that the rest of our customers will be interested in?"

"We've got mountains of customer information lying about, but what part of this information contains the business-critical knowledge that can teach us to send relevant campaigns to relevant customers?" Data-driven analytics are relevant here, because we do not know which data we should be examining first. We obviously have some pretty good ideas about this, but no actual knowledge. We have another problem which is that next month when we prepare our campaign, we'll be none the wiser. Our customer information has been updated since last time, and the campaign is a different one.

It makes sense, too, to look at our internal competencies and analytical tools. If we look at the problem from a broader perspective, it is, of course, possible that we will not choose a data mining solution, because it might be an isolated exercise that will require relatively large investments.

If you have now decided that you need the hypothesis-driven approach, you can proceed to the next section. Likewise, you can proceed to the next question if you feel confident that the data-driven types of analytics are the right ones for you. If you are still not sure, because the knowledge you want to generate can be created in both ways, you simply have a choice. You should consider which of the two requires fewer resources and is more accessible to the user. Note that most data mining tools can automate large parts of the process. So if you have an analysis that is going to be repeated many times, this can render some significant benefits. Equally, you could consider whether you can kill more birds with one stone. A data mart that is developed to be able to identify which customers will leave you when and why will also be useful in other contexts and will therefore render considerable time savings in connection with ad hoc tasks. Thus a simple question such as which segments purchase which products can be answered in as little as five minutes, when reusing the data mining mart as a regular customer mart. The alternative response time would be hours, because it involves making the SQL from scratch, merging the information, and validating the results.

Question 3: Determine whether the data-driven method has the objective of examining the correlation between one given dependent variable and a large number of other variables, or whether the objective is to identify different kinds of structures in data. If we begin by describing situations where we have a target variable, we would want to describe this variable via a model. We could be an insurance company that has collected data via test samples about which claims are fraudulent and which are true. Based on this information, we can train a model to understand when we have a fraudulent claim and when we don't. From that point forward, the model can systematically help us identify and follow up on past as well as future cases that are suspicious,. We therefore have a target variable—"Was it fraudulent?" "Or was it not?"—and a number of other variables that we can use to build a model. These variables might describe factors such as which type of damage, under which circumstances, which types of people report them, have there been frequent claims, and so on.

A target variable might also be the right price of a house. If we are a mortgage lender, we can make a model based on historical prices, which illustrates the correlations between the price of the house and factors such as location, size, when it was built, and so forth. This means we can ask our customers about these factors and calculate the value of the house and the derived security it constitutes for us as lenders, thus saving us sending a person out to evaluate it.

Another target variable might be customer satisfaction. If we send out a questionnaire to a large number of customers and then divide the customers into groups according to satisfaction level, we can make a model that combines satisfaction scores with our internal data warehouse information about the customers. We can then train the model in understanding the correlations and, based on the model, we can score all the customers that did not complete the questionnaire. We then end up with an estimated satisfaction score, which we can use as a good substitute.

As opposed to data mining techniques that build on target variables, we now see a large number of analytical techniques that look for patterns in data. The techniques that we have included here are techniques for data reduction. These are typically used if we have a large number of variables with little information, and we want to reduce the number of variables to a smaller number of variables (without losing the information value) and interpret and isolate different kinds of information. For example, we might have a survey with 50 questions about our business, and we know that there are only three to five things that really matter to the customers. These techniques can then tell us how many factors actually mean something to our customers and what these factors are.

Cluster analysis can also divide customers into comparable groups based on patterns in data. We do not know beforehand how many homogeneous groups or clusters we've got, but the model can tell us this, along with their characteristics, and can also make a segmentation of our customers based on the model.

Cross-sales and up-sales models also look for patterns in data, and can provide us with answers to questions about which products customers typically buy in combination, and how their needs develop over time. They make use of many different types of more or less statistical algorithms, but are characterized by not developing through learning about the correlation between one single variable and a large number of others. As a supplement to these models, data mining models with target variables work well, where the target variable describes those who have purchased a given product compared with those who haven't. The rest of the customer information is then used to gain a profile of the differences between the two groups.

Following the discussion of the three imperatives that must be considered in order to identify which information domain to use in connection with the information strategy, we will now go through the general methods we've chosen to include. We want to emphasize once again that this is not a complete list of all existing methods, nor is this a book about statistics. What we are listing are the most frequently used methods in BA.

Descriptive Statistical Methods, Lists, and Reports

If you answered yes to data manager or report developer or controller competencies previously (see Exhibit 4.2, Question 1), this section will provide you with more detail.

Since popular terminology distinguishes between lists, which the sales department, for instance, uses to make their calls and reports, and which typically show some aggregated numeric information (averages, numbers, share, etc.), we have chosen to make the same distinction in our heading. Technically speaking, it doesn't make much difference whether the cells in the table consist of a long list of names or some calculated figures. In the following, we will simply refer to them as reports, as an overall term for these types of deliveries.

We have chosen to define reporting in a BA context as, "selection and presentation of information, which is left to the end user to interpret and act on." From a statistical perspective, we call this *descriptive statistics*; information is merely presented, no hypothesis tests or explorative analyses of data structures are performed.

This form of transfer of information to customers is by far the most common in companies, because after a number of standard reports are established, they can be automated. Ad hoc projects are different because they require the investment of human resources in the process each time. Moreover, if we look at the typical definition of BA, "to ensure that the right users receive the right information at the right time," this describes what we typically want to get from a technical BA solution in the short run. This also tells us about the most common purpose of having a technical data warehouse and a reporting solution (i.e., to collect information with a view to turning it into reports). We also control users' reading access to these reports through their access. Finally, we ensure that reports are updated according to some rule (e.g., once a month). Alternatively, the reports might be conditional, which means that they are updated and the users are advised of this, if certain conditions are met. These might be conditions such as a customer displaying a particular behavior, and the customer executive is therefore informed of this behavior along with key figures. Alternatively, as is known in business activity monitoring (BAM), in cases where certain critical values are exceeded, the report on this process is then updated and the process owner is informed.

Ad Hoc Reports

Ad hoc reports are the type of delivery required by the customer if we have information that we need in connection with, for instance, a business case or a suspicion or critical question that must be confirmed or denied. We might, for instance, have a suspicion that the public sector segment rejects certain products that we produce, and we therefore need a report on this particular problem.

The procedure when establishing this type of project is completely straightforward and is based on the recipient in the business, as a minimum, designing the table he or she requires. The advantage is that the recipient contemplates which information he or she needs and in which form. Will averages suffice, or are variance targets needed? Revenue might have to be broken down into categories from 0 to 100, 100 to 200, and above, and then we just need to know how many customers exist in each category. Besides, there might well be a number of considerations concerning which data to build the analysis on. In connection with the above example where we divide the customer into categories, we might consider whether to include semipublic institutions such as sport centers or independent institutions in our analysis. And does the analysis apply only to companies that are not in a dunning process, and that have been active customers with us for the past two years? It might seem like a lengthy process, but this kind of requirement specification ensures that the first delivery from the analyst is correct. As most analysts will know, there are two kinds of internal customers; the ones you can perform a task for in one attempt, and the ones with whom you need to go through at least three attempts.

Manually Updated Reports

Manually updated reports are normally used in connection with projects and therefore have a limited lifetime. This short-term value makes it financially unviable to put these reports into regular production. Alternatively, the reports might come about because certain users do not have access to the company's reporting systems or simply can't make sense of them.

Other times these reports are chosen as a solution because their requirements keep changing, or the dimensions change. Poor data quality might also be at the root of this, a table that might need manual sorting every time, or that the analyst can add some knowledge to. Finally, there might be technical reasons why the business can't deliver anything apart from this type of reports. It is not an unknown phenomenon, either, for analysts to train executives to hand over reports in person—for the sake of attention!

Even though the reports are typically initiated on a project basis, they do have a tendency to become a regular delivery. When the business user has worked with the report, it's only natural that he or she would like to be able to see some useful purposes in this new perspective and request this on an ongoing basis of, say, once a month. In principle, this is fine. It simply confirms that the BA function is delivering useful information. However, there are other things to take into consideration.

It's a question of resources. An analyst's time is precious. The more time an analyst spends on preparing a report the less he or she has for other projects. It is not uncommon for an analyst to be almost drowning in his or her own success. Specifically, this means that we have an analyst who uses all his or her time at work on updating standard reports, which he or she once created for the users. If we let this continue, two things will happen. First, we achieve no further development of the knowledge that the analyst could otherwise contribute. Second, the entire information flow in the company stops, when the analyst changes jobs because he or she has had enough of all the routine tasks.

In a broader organizational context, this kind of ungoverned reporting inevitably brings about different reporting conditions and thereby different versions of the same truth. Some people in the organization will know more than others, and these people will exchange information, and the organization thus establishes different levels of knowledge. Another consequence of this kind of ungoverned reporting is that the investments that were made in an automated reporting system will become more or less superfluous.

The solution to this conflict between analysts and the people responsible for the automated reporting systems is not that the analysts refuse to prepare repeat reports, but that continuous transfers of reports to automated systems take place. The analyst could receive a guarantee from those responsible for the automated processes that they will generate all standard reports. However, there are reports that are so complex that they cannot be fully automated. There might be some estimated decisions in connection with forecast, which the analyst needs to relate to—as we know, there are no rules without exceptions. In any event, it could still be discussed whether it should be the user of the report who does the calculation, and have the automated processes support him or her as best they can.

Automated Reports: On Demand

This type of report is typically delivered in connection with data warehouse implementations and is based on users having access to a multitude of information that is updated on a regular basis.

There are no routines in place, however, as to whether those who have access actually read the reports, which is what is meant by the expression on demand (only when the user requests it). Typically, the technical solution consists of an individualized user interface, controlled by the user's login, which ensures that the user views relevant information only, and that any personal information (e.g., salary and illness) is not publically accessible in the organization.

One of the advantages of most types of automated reports is that they are not static. Most of them are interactive, which means that the user can drill down into the details by breaking down a given report into further dimensions. If we have a report describing revenue in the different national regions, we can ask the report to break down sales into which stores sold for how much, or which product groups generated which revenue. When talking about interactive reports, we can more specifically say that we gain access to a multitude of data or a data domain (the revenue), which provides users with the opportunity to analyze via a number of dimensions (regions, stores, products, etc.). For details about dimensions, see Chapter 5. The visualization of reports is something we will typically get from most front-end solutions, where a front-end is the user interface to the technical solution. So we are not only getting table reports, but we can also visualize this information, which can be an extremely time-saving function, for instance, in connection with reports that perform general monitoring of market trends over time. A graph typically gives a better overview of trends than does a series of numbers (see Chapter 5 for more).

Automated Reports: Event Driven

This type of report works like the *on-demand* reports, with the one difference that they remind the user when to read them. The event that triggers a report can be anything from the passing of a time interval to the fact that some critical values have been exceeded in data. When it's a case of time intervals being exceeded, there is not much difference between this reporting form and the on-demand reporting form, where we must assume that the report is read at regular intervals. In cases where certain critical values are exceeded, the report starts representing an alarm, too. If, in connection with production reports, for instance, we discover that over 3% of the produced items have errors, the report will first of all sound the alarm to the production executive, and at the same time give him or her opportunity to react quickly.

In continuation of the lag information in an information strategy, a useful way of using this type of reporting would be in connection with investigating whether some of the established key performance indicators (KPIs) were over or under a critical level. Levels are often already defined in connection with KPI reporting in order that the technical solution, which automates the reporting, can put on so-called traffic lights or smileys, which show whether a process is on track or not. The advantage of such a solution is that the report itself contacts its users when problems occur so that these can be solved at short notice, rather than users discovering these problems at the end of the month, when the new figures are published.

Event-driven reporting is thought to have a great future, a future in which relevant information presents itself to the individual user at the right time. In fact, that is something that we are able to do already to some extent. But the instance where the underlying intelligence is specifying what is the right information at the right time will become much more refined as described in Chapter 9, which covers pervasive BA.

Reports in General

In previous sections, we discussed the difference between lead and lag information, and pointed out that lag information will typically be distributed via reports. This means that it must be a requirement that an information strategy includes a set of reports that, via the measuring of

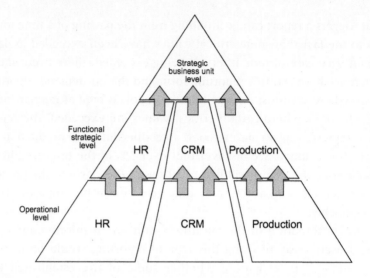

EXHIBIT 4.3 Demands to the Reporting are Hierarchically and Internally Aligned

critical business processes, is able to provide support for the chosen business strategy. This also means that the reports taken together both cover an area and at the same time are mutually exclusive. Our processes will thus be monitored and we will know precisely who is responsible for any corrective actions.

This means that we need the reports to be able to report to each other at higher as well as lower levels, as illustrated in Exhibit 4.3. If we have a report, for instance, describing monthly sales figures and a report showing daily sales figures, we need to be able to balance both internally. This brings about a need for one central data warehouse that feeds both reports. It stands to reason that if one report is built on figures from the finance department and another is built from information from daily aggregated till reports, the two reports can never be balanced. It is therefore important that we understand that we must choose one version of the truth, when establishing a reporting system, even though we could easily define many. Equally, consistency is crucial when choosing the dimensions for generating the reports. If we break down the monthly reports in regions, we must break down the corresponding daily reports into the same regions.

HYPOTHESIS-DRIVEN METHODS

When working with hypothesis-driven methods, we use statistical tests to examine the relationship between some variables in, let's say, gender and age. The result of the test will be a number between 0 and 1, describing the risks of our being wrong, if we conclude based on the data material that there is a relationship between gender and lifetime. The rule is then that if the value we find is under 0.05, that is, 5%, then the likelihood of our being wrong is so insignificant that we will conclude that there is a relationship. However, this means that if we perform 20 tests between variables that have nothing to do with each other, then we can, based on an average perspective, still show a statistical correlation $(1/0.05 = 20)$. This is why it's a general requirement that we do not just hold all sorts of variables up against each other, but that we must have some initial idea of the relationship. This doesn't change the fact, of course, that every twentieth time a test is performed between two variables that have nothing to do with each other, a statistically significant relationship will be found anyway, but it does remove some of the incorrect knowledge we would otherwise be generating.

In a BA context, this means that if we want knowledge about our customers, we first have to go through a process of identifying which variables we want to include in the analysis as well as which relations between the variables it makes sense to test. This is exemplified in Exhibit 4.4, where statistics in a BA context are typically about identifying the relevant data and testing for relevant correlations. Based on identified significant relationships between the variables, we can make an overall description as a conclusion on our analysis.

Tests with Several Input Variables

There are tests that can handle several input variables at a time. The advantage of these tests is that they can reveal any synergies between the input variables. This is relevant if, for instance, a company is contemplating changing its pricing of a product and combining this change with a sales campaign. Both these steps are likely to have a positive effect on sales, but supposed there is a cumulative effect in undertaking the two initiatives at the same time. It is not enough,

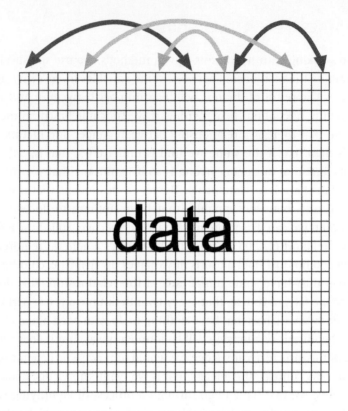

EXHIBIT 4.4   Illustration of Tests between Two Variables in Our Datasets

therefore, to carry out two tests; one that shows the correlation between price and sales of a product and one that shows campaign
launch and sales on the same product. In fact, we need to investigate a
third dimension (e.g., what are the synergies between price reduction
and campaign launch on the one hand and sales on the other?).

Which test to choose depends on the dependent variable (the dependent variable is the variable that we want to learn something
about) which in the previous example is sales. In the field of statistics,
we distinguish strongly between the scaling of the dependent variable,
as this determines which method to use. If we are after some estimates
(interval-dependent variable), this could be in connection with the
need for knowledge about the correlation between the price of a house
on the one hand, and everything that determines this price on the

other (how old it is, its last renovation, number of square meters, size of overall property, insulation, etc.).

The variable we want to know something about is characterized by the fact that it makes sense to look at its average—that is, to multiply or divide it. The most commonly used method in this context is called *linear regression analysis*, and it describes the correlation between an interval variable and a number of input variables. Forecasting techniques, which look for correlations over time, would also typically be in this category. Forecasting techniques are based on looking at the correlation between, say, sales over time and a large number of input variables, such as price level, our own and others' campaigns, product introductions, seasons, and so on. Based on this correlation, we can conclude which factors determine sales over time, whether there are any synergies between these factors and how much of a delay there is before they take effect. If we are running a TV commercial, when do we see its effect on sales, and how long does its effect last? If we have this information, we can subsequently begin to plan our campaigns in such a way that we achieve maximum effect per invested marketing dollar.

Forecasting is thus used for two things: (1) to create projection of trends, and (2) to learn from historical correlations. Forecasting methods are therefore extremely valuable tools in terms of optimizing processes, where we want to know, based on KPIs, how we can best optimize our performance. Sales campaigns utilize these methods because the companies need to measure which customers got their message. This is well-known for companies investing in TV commercials who only know how many commercial slots they've bought, and where they want to perform a subsequent measuring of any effect on sales. In addition, forecasting models play an important role here in explaining the synergies among different advertising media, such as radio, TV, and billboards, so that we can find the optimum combination.

If we want to create profiles (binary-dependent variables, which means that there are only two outcomes; e.g., "Yes or No," and "New customer profile or Old customer profile") using BA information, this might be a case of wanting a profile on the new customers we get in relation to our old ones, or an analysis of which employees gave notice in the last year. What we want is to disclose which input variables might contribute to describe the differences between Group A and Group B, where Group A and B, respectively, are the dependent variable. If we take the example of employees leaving the business in the last year, there might be information such as age, gender, seniority, absence due to illness, and so forth that might describe the difference between the two groups. In this context, the method that is typically used is a binary regression analysis.

In some cases, we want to explain how the variables rank (ordinal-dependent variables), because we want to know more about satisfaction scores, where the satisfaction score will typically be called something like "very happy," "happy," "neutral," "unhappy," or "very unhappy." A rank variable is therefore characterized by a given number of optional answers that are ranked, but where we cannot average them. Although many people code the ranked variables from 1 to 5, it is statistically and methodically wrong to do so.

If we, for instance, want to understand which of our customers are very satisfied with our customer service, we could look at the correlation between gender, age, education, history, and then their satisfaction score using a method called *ordinal regression analysis*. A similar analysis must be used if, as in another example, we want to analyze our customer segments, and if these segments are value segmented and thereby rankable.

Finally, if we want to understand something about a group we would use a nominal-dependent variable. Maybe we have some regional differences or certain groups of employees that we want to understand better. We can't just rank regions, and say that Denmark ranks better than Norway, and then Sweden is third. One analysis could focus on the different characteristics of our customers in the Norwegian, Danish, and Swedish markets, where our input variables could be gender, age, education, and purchasing history. In this case, we would typically use a generalized linear model (GLM) analysis.

DATA MINING WITH TARGET VARIABLES

Data mining reveals correlations and patterns in data by means of predictive techniques. These correlations and patterns are critical to decision making, because they disclose areas for process improvement.

By using data mining, the organization can, for instance, increase the profitability of its interaction with customers. Patterns that are found using data mining technology help the organization make better decisions. Data mining is a data-driven process. A data mining project often takes several weeks to carry out, partly because we are often talking about large volumes of data (both rows and columns) as input for the models. This is true even though the development in computer power has shortened this process considerably, and partly because we would probably want to automate the process so that it can be performed in a matter of hours next time. To perform this task, it's essential to have specialized data mining software that is managed by analysts rather than conventional data warehouse people. We also recommend that companies choose a software vendor who offers courses in the use of their software. Any course fees have a quick return, if data mining is being performed for the first time.

Exhibit 4.5 shows the data mining process in three steps: (1) creating a number of models, (2) selecting the best model, and (3) using the selected model.

The City of Copenhagen Municipality needed to find out which employees had stress or long-term absence due to illness. The first step, therefore, included collecting a large amount of historical information about absences due to illness, pay level, organizational level, labor agreement, and so forth. In addition, we had information about who had had a long-term absence and at what time. We were therefore able to create two groups: (1) those who had not had a long absence due to illness, and (2) those who had had a long absence within that time. By means of a number of algorithms (neural network, decision trees, and binary regression analyses, used here in a data mining context), we came up with profiles of the differences between the two groups, and thereby characterized those employees who had a long absence due to illness. The result was that we had a number of models, and it was impossible to say that one would definitely be better than the other, since they had been developed in different ways.

The purpose of the second step (selecting the best model) is to identify which model is going to render the best results on an unknown dataset. An "unknown" dataset has the same characteristics as the original dataset on which the model was developed. This ensures

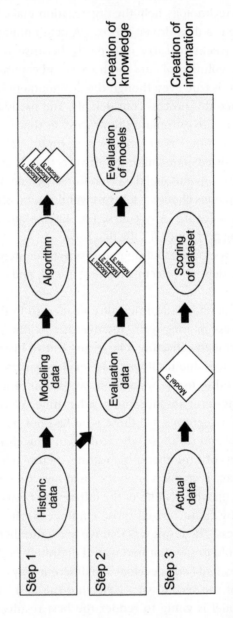

EXHIBIT 4.5 The Three Steps of a Data Mining Process

that the model we choose will not only be the best to describe the dataset on which it has been developed, but can be generalized and applied to other datasets. In relation to the City of Copenhagen Municipality in Denmark, this ensured that not only was the model able to explain the historical absence due to illness in the dataset on which it was based, but the model was also able to come up with good results on current datasets and thereby deliver efficient predictions on the dataset it would be used on in future. The way we performed the testing was to let the model predict whether each of the profiles in the unknown dataset would enter into a long absence due to illness. We then related this information with whether the employees described in the historical dataset did actually become ill, and therefore we were able to see which of the models were best at explaining the general tendencies underlying long-term illness in the City of Copenhagen Municipality.

When we reach this stage in the process, we can begin interpreting the models. Depending on the different types of algorithms, it varies a lot how much we are able to interpret; nevertheless, this step gives us the opportunity to generate knowledge about the problem at hand. (See Exhibit 4.6.) Later in this chapter, we'll look at which methods provide access to which types of knowledge.

The third step in the process is to create one-to-one information on which to act. In the case of the City of Copenhagen Municipality, we had the opportunity to work with a current dataset, identical to the

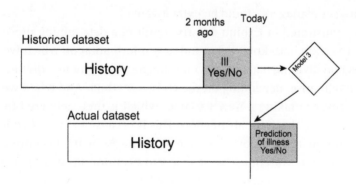

EXHIBIT 4.6 History Is Used to Make Predictions about Illness in the City of Copenhagen Municipality

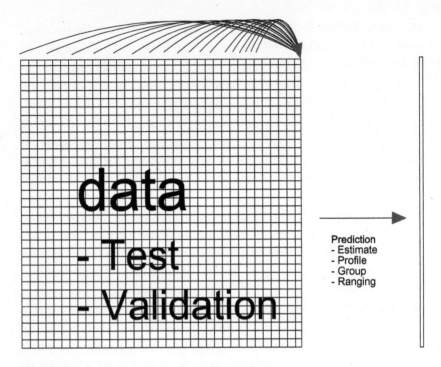

EXHIBIT 4.7　Prediction Using the Data Mining Method

historical dataset, only more recent, and so we didn't know who would get ill. The model was able to identify employees with an increased risk of entering into a long absence due to illness in the coming period of time, and the model could therefore inform us about which specific employees managers should be extra aware of.

As illustrated in Exhibit 4.7, the result of a data mining process is that we create both knowledge and new information on which we can act. When dividing data into several subgroups, even more divisions of data might arise, depending on the chosen method. And when we describe this as making a new variable, which is then delivered to our users as a list, this is an abstraction. This is because we are often looking to automate the information creation process by implementing the model in a data warehouse with a view to a continuous scoring of data, and an action is automatically executed based on the model.

One example could be a solution that the authors made for a large telecom company. Based on information found in the customer relationship management (CRM) system of the company's call center, we found a number of clear correlations between the inquiries from corporate customers and whether they canceled their subscriptions shortly after. These inquiries could be about whether they could get a discount, or whether they could get a good deal on some new phones, as the old ones were getting quite worn. The questions were clear indications of customers on a quest, and that they should be contacted immediately by a person with great experience in corporate solutions. Consequently, we created a data mining model to identify the most important danger signals. Based on the model, an automated electronic service was generated that scanned the data warehouse of the call center every five minutes. If any "critical" calls were found in the log readings from conversations with customers—which could be that they had called in for a good deal combined with the fact that their contract was up—then the person who was responsible for this customer would automatically receive an email. With reference to the reporting section of this chapter, this is essentially an event driven report which is generated based on a data mining algorithm.

What we see in the call center example is what those in process optimization call an externally executed action, which means that it's not us, but something else, that initiates a process. In this case, it's a critical call. In connection with the ongoing accumulation of information about the customers in a market that reacts ever faster, this is a trend we will probably see more of in the future. It already exists on a small scale in so-called marketing automation programs, so much so that when a customer changes her surname it is assumed that she has gotten married and therefore is sent an offer for family insurance. Similarly, if a new address is registered on a store Web site, certain programs will calculate where the nearest store is and automatically send out an email with this information. This is all the beginnings of what is called *pervasive business analytics*, which is built on you and me, based on our behavior and other information, receiving relevant information, when it is assumed that we need it. We will discuss pervasive business analytics in detail in Chapter 9.

Data Mining Algorithms

In the field of statistics, a precedent has been established for choosing which specific statistical methods or algorithms to use based on the data we are holding in one hand and the conclusion we would like to be holding in the other. In data mining, there is a tendency to prefer the model that will render the best results on an unknown dataset (i.e., the model that can generate the best new column for predictive purposes, as shown in Exhibit 4.7). In the following section, we will therefore go through the most popular techniques and group them according to the types of problems they can solve.

The purpose of data mining with a target variable will always be to explain this target variable. It is comparable to a statistical test, where we have a dependent variable and many explanatory ones. The only difference is terminology, where data mining uses the terms *target variable* and *input variables*. As with statistics, our target variables, and thus what we are trying to explain and predict, might be an estimate, a profile, a ranking, or a grouping.

The business problems covered by the four types of target variables have already been explained in the section of this chapter titled "Tests with Several Input Variables." The most common techniques are neural networks and decision trees. Neural networks are characterized by being fast to work with. They do have the significant weakness, however, of being practically impossible to interpret and communicate because of their high level of complexity. Decision trees are easier to interpret and have the added advantage of being interactive, giving the analyst the scope for constant adaptation of the model, according to what he or she thinks will improve the results. Interactive decision trees can be compared with online analytical processing (OLAP) cubes or pivot tables, where the analyst can continue to drill deeper and deeper into the required dimensions. The analyst constantly receives decision support in the form of statistical information about the significant or incidental nature of the discovered differences. In our telecom case study at BA-support.com, we give an example of how to use and read a decision tree.

Various kinds of regression analyses are used in data mining, too. The methods are typically developed in the same way as in the statistics field, but in a data mining context, the models are evaluated on an equal footing with decision trees and neural networks based on whether they are able to deliver efficient predictions in unknown datasets.

EXPLORATIVE METHODS

In BA, we typically see four types of explorative analyses. These are methods for data reduction, cluster analysis, cross-sell models, and up-sell models.

In connection with explorative models, we leave it to the algorithms to discover tendencies in the data material. The methods are therefore data driven, but there are no target variables that we want to model. Consequently, there is no way to conduct quality assurance testing on our models by testing them on unknown datasets. The quality assurance typically consists of the analysts evaluating whether the identified patterns make sense, which is the reverse of what we know from statistics, and where the theory precedes the test.

Another way of assuring the quality of our models is, for example, to let the same algorithm make a model on another and similar dataset and, if the algorithm comes up with the same model, we can presume that it is not a coincidence in the given data material in combination with the algorithm that gives the result. Alternatively, we could let two different algorithms analyze a dataset and, if they produce comparable solutions, we could presume that it is the result of some underlying patterns in the data and not a coincidence in the interaction between the individual algorithm and the dataset.

Data Reduction

The reason for performing data reduction might seem somewhat abstract, but data reduction does have its advantages, as we will show in the following section. In specific terms, we take all the information in a large number of variables and condense it into a smaller number of variables.

In the field of statistics, data reduction is used in connection with analyses of questionnaire information, where we've got a large number of questions that are actually disclosing information only about a smaller number of factors. Instead of a questionnaire with, say, 20 questions about all kinds of things, we can identify how many dimensions are of interest to our customers and then ask about just these. We could therefore move from measuring customer satisfaction using 20 variables to measuring only the five variables that most precisely express our customers' needs. These five new variables will also have the advantage of having no internal correlation. That is ideal input for a subsequent cluster analysis, where many variables sharing the same information (high correlation) affect the clustering model in a way that we do not want.

Data reduction is typically used when there are many variables that each contain little information that is relevant in terms of what we need. Using this method, we can try to condense the information into a smaller number of variables, in the hope that the new variables now contain a concentrate of relevant information, and that this can make a positive difference. The most popular method for data reduction is principal component analysis (PCA), which is also called explorative factor analysis. The correspondence analysis is also quite commonly used.

Cluster Analysis

Other types of explorative analyses, which are frequently used in BA, are cluster analyses. Instead of working with a very large number of individual customers, we can produce an easy-to-see number of segments, or clusters, for observation. There are numerous methods for this, but they all basically focus on algorithms to combine observations that are similar. In statistics, cluster analyses are typically used to investigate whether there are any natural groupings in the data, in which case analyses can be performed on separate clusters, while data mining will typically use the identified cluster, if this improves predictability in the model they are to be included in. Finally, the purpose of the analysis might be the segmentation per se, as this will give us an indication of how we can make some natural divisions of segments based on information about our customers' response and consumption.

In terms of the relationship between data reduction and cluster analyses, data reduction facilitates the process of reducing a large number of variables to a smaller number. The cluster analysis also simplifies data structures by reducing a large number of rows of individual customers to a smaller number of segments. For this exact reason, the two methods are often used in combination with questionnaires, where data reduction identifies the few dimensions that are of great significance, and the cluster analysis then divides the respondents into homogenous groups.

Cross-Sell Models

Cross-sell models are also known as basket analysis models. These models will show which products people typically buy together. For instance, if we find that people who buy red wine frequently buy cheese and crackers, too, it makes sense to place these products next to each other in the store. This type of model is also used in connection with combined offers. They are used, too, when a company places related pieces of information next to each other on its Web site, so that if a customer wants to look at cameras, he or she will find some offers on electronic storage media, too. Amazon.com is a case in point: If a user wants to look at a book, he or she will at the same time be presented with a large number of other relevant books. The other "relevant" books are selected on the basis of historical knowledge about which books other users have purchased in addition to the book the customer is looking at.

Up-Sell Models

Up-sell models are used when a company wants to create more sales per customer by giving the individual customer the right offer at the right time. These models are based on the notion that a kind of con-sumption cycle exists. A time perspective has been added here. We are not looking at what's in the shopping basket once; instead, we are looking at the contents of the shopping basket over time. If, for exam-ple, we find that people who at one point have had one kind of sofa will get another specific sofa at a later stage, we will want to promote the new type of sofa with suitable intervals after the first sofa has been purchased. This way of "developing" customers is known from bank-ing products, too, where customers have a relatively fixed life cycle with youth account, family account, children's savings account to grandchildren's savings account and finally a pensioner's savings account. In the software industry, the method is used to discover who will buy upgrades of software at an early stage. Based on this information, a vendor can endeavor to penetrate the market with new versions.

BUSINESS REQUIREMENTS

Imagine an analyst or a controller from a business analytics department who sits at a desk looking a colleague from a business-oriented function in the eye. The business user asks, "So what can you do for me?" There are, of course, plenty of good answers to this excellent question, as we shall see later in this chapter. One point that is crucial for the analyst to make, however, is, "I can deliver business requirements."

Business requirements is a kind of interpreting and communicating task that is a substantial part of an analyst's tool kit. Furthermore, it's a "shelf product" in most large consultancy firms. The requirement for the analyst is to be able to understand and translate the business user's thoughts and needs into something that can be answered through analyst or data manager or report developer competencies. The purpose is to deliver something that can be used by the business to improve processes, and which corresponds with the business strategy as well.

Producing business requirements requires a sound knowledge of business issues and processes as well as insight into the company's data warehouse and other IT infrastructure. As previously mentioned, one of the analyst's key competencies is to be able to build a bridge between business process and the technical environment. He or she has, so to speak, a foot in each camp, as illustrated in the BA model from Chapter 1. A good point of departure for the delivery of business requirements is a thorough interview, where the business user is interviewed by the analyst from the business analytics department. Business requirements can be built in many ways. In this book, we use a three-tier structure, which includes definition of the overall problem, definition of delivery, and definition of content.

Definition of the Overall Problem

Based on this definition, the analyst must be able to place the specific task in a broader context, and thereby prioritize it in relation to other tasks. Consequently, the commissioner of the task must be able to explain for which business processes the given task will be adding value, if the task is to be prioritized based on a business case. Alternatively, the commissioner must relate the task to a strategic initiative. Otherwise, the analyst must be extremely careful in taking on the task, because if it's not adding value, and not related to the business strategy, he or she must question the justification of the task.

Definition of Delivery

The requesting party (recipient) must specify in which media the analysis must be delivered (HTML, PDF, Excel, PowerPoint, Word, etc.) and whether the delivery must include an explanation of the results, or whether these are self-explanatory.

Deliveries that include automated processes, such as on-demand reports or continuous lists of customers to call, need to have a clear agreement on roles and responsibilities. Who shall have access to the reports, or who is the list to be sent to in sales? Similarly, an owner of the reports must specify, either as a function or a person, who is responsible for ensuring that the business requirements are based on the BA information, and who is to be notified of any errors, changes, or breakdown in the automated delivery. The reason for this is that automated reports are not a static entity; changes might be made to the data foundation on which they are built, which means that they are no longer structured in the optimum way. In addition, the technology on which they are built might be phased out. Errors are inevitable over time but if effective communication is in place, damage to business procedures can be prevented. The question is not whether an incorrect report will be delivered at some stage or not, because that is to be expected; the question is how efficiently we deal with the situation when it arises.

Other questions to clarify about delivery is time of delivery (on demand), or under which circumstances we update (event driven), and whether to notify users when updating.

Definition of Content

In connection with report solutions the content part of a BA project is very concrete, since it is about designing the layout as well as defining the data foundation. As mentioned in the section about on-demand reports, this type of report is not just a static document, but a dynamic data domain—it could be sales figures—that we want to break down into a number of dimensions, such as by salesperson, department, area, or product type. Often users experience problems grasping this new functionality. However, we have to remember to train users in how to work with the dynamic reporting tool, too.

Data quality is a subject that needs discussing, also, since our data warehouse contains imprecise or incorrect information, which we have chosen to live with for various reasons. What is the acceptable level of accuracy? Can we live with a margin of error of 5% between the daily reporting and the monthly figures from the finance department? In cases where we don't have the desired information quality in our data warehouse, this question is essential, since it determines how many resources we must use to sort out our data, before we dare to make decisions based on the derived reports. A company must know the quality of its data, and either live with it or do something about it. Unfortunately, we often experience that data quality is known as being poor and the data warehouse is therefore unused. That is an unfortunate waste of resources.

In Exhibit 4.8 we have given an example of how a company may use a mind map to collect the relevant information in connection with business requirements for the reporting solution from the radio station case study in Chapter 1.

For tasks that, to a great extent, require quantitative analytical competencies, a business performance specification will take the form of an ongoing dialogue. Unlike reports where the user interprets the results, in this specification the analyst will be doing the interpretation of quantitative analytical tasks. Naturally, this means that unforeseen

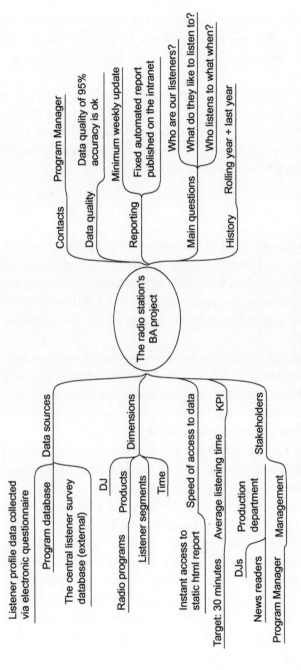

EXHIBIT 4.8 Business Requirements for the Radio Station Case Study (Chapter 1), Visualized with a Mind Map

133

problems might be encountered in the process. These must be discussed and dealt with. The initial preparation of business requirements
must state clearly who possesses business key competencies for
answering any questions, and then make sure that these people are
available as needed.

Similarly, in connection with major projects, such as data mining
solutions, certain subtargets should be agreed on to facilitate a continuous evaluation of whether the performance of the overall task is on
track in relation to its potential value creation as well as whether more
resources and competencies should be added.

SUMMARY

In this chapter, we have looked at the analyst's role in the BA model,
which was defined in Chapter 1. The analyst is a bridge builder
between the company and its technical environment. Purchasing BA
software is not sufficient to secure successful BA initiatives; the
company must take care to invest in the human aspect of its information system as well.

Generally speaking, the analyst possesses business insight, technical insight, and the ability to choose the correct methodical approach
and presentation form. In other words, the analyst's tool kit must be in
order. And there is a fourth item for the list of competencies: the analyst's ability to deliver a business requirements document.

We have looked at the four information domains in the analyst's
methodical field and suggested when it is beneficial to deploy these
for performing various tasks. The descriptive statistical information
domain is the typical work area for the typical analyst, and it is usually
presented to users in reports. We have discussed different forms of
reports. However, it is characteristic of this method that the individual
viewer or business user will be the person to interpret and transfer this
information into knowledge. In other words, users themselves have to
create knowledge from the information, which means that absolute
knowledge in the information domain is not being created, but rather
relative knowledge. These tasks are performed wearing the controller
hat (data manager or report developer competencies).

The analyst creates absolute knowledge in the information domains: statistical tests, data mining, and explorative analytics. These analytical methods are used for creating knowledge about correlations between variables and identifying patterns in data in order to be able to predict, for instance, the scope for cross-selling and up-selling. The presented information from these methodical processes is not meant to be subsequently interpreted and transferred into knowledge by individual business users, because these analytical results are indisputable.

CHAPTER 5

Business Analytics at the Data Warehouse Level

I n Chapter 4, we looked at the processes that transform raw warehouse data into information and knowledge. Later on, in Chapter 6, we will look at the typical data-creating source systems that constitute the real input to a data warehouse.

In this chapter, we discuss how to store data to best support business processes and thereby the request for value creation. We'll look at the advantages of having a data warehouse and explain the architecture and processes in a data warehouse. We look briefly at the concept of master data management, too, and touch upon service-oriented architecture (SOA). Finally, we discuss the approaches to be adopted by analysts and business users to different parts of a data warehouse, based on which information domain they wish to use.

WHY A DATA WAREHOUSE?

The point of having a data warehouse is to give the organization a common information platform, which ensures consistent, integrated, and valid data across source systems and business areas. This is essential if a company wants to obtain the most complete picture possible of its customers.

In order to gather information about our customers from many different systems to generate a 360-degree profile based on the information we have about our customers already, we have to join information from a large number of independent systems, such as:

- Billing systems (systems printing bills)
- Reminder systems (systems sending out reminders, if customers do not pay on time, and credit scores)
- Debt collection systems (status on cases that were outsourced for external collection)
- Customer relationship management (CRM) systems (systems for storing history about customer meetings and calls)
- Product and purchasing information (which products and services a customer has purchased over time)
- Customer information (names, addresses, opening of accounts, cancellations, special contracts, segmentations, etc.)
- Corporate information (industry codes, number of employees, accounts figures)
- Campaign history (who received which campaigns and when)
- Web logs (information about customer behavior on our portals)
- Various questionnaire surveys carried out over time
- Human resources information (information about employees, time sheets, their competencies, and history)
- Production information (production processes, inventory management, procurement)
- Generation of key performance indicators (KPIs; used for monitoring current processes, but can be used to optimize processes at a later stage)
- Data mining results (segmentations, added sales models, loyalty segmentations, up-sales models, loyalty segmentations, all of which have their history added when they are placed in a data warehouse)

As shown, the business analytics (BA) function receives input from different primary source systems and combines and uses these in a different context than initially intended. A billing system, for instance, was built to send out bills, and when they have been sent, it's up to the reminder system to monitor whether reminders should be sent out. Consequently, we might as well delete the information about the bills that were sent to customers, if we don't want to use it in other contexts. Other contexts might be: profit and loss, preparing accounts, monitoring sales, value-based segmentation or activity-based costing activities—contexts that require the combination of information about customers across our primary systems over time and that make this data available to the organization's analytical competencies. Business analytics is not possible without access to a combined data foundation from the organization's data-creating source systems. In fact, that is exactly what a data warehouse does.

A data warehouse consists of a technical part and a business part. The technical part must ensure that the organization's data is collected from its source systems, and that it is stored, combined, structured, and cleansed regardless of the source system platform. The business content of a data warehouse must ensure that the desired key figures and reports can be created.

There are many good arguments for integrating data into an overall data warehouse, including:

- To avoid information islands and manual processes in connection with the organization's primary systems.
- To avoid overloading of source systems with daily reporting and analysis.
- To integrate data from many different source systems.
- To create a historical data foundation that can be changed/ removed in source systems (e.g., saving the orders historically, even if the enterprise resource planning [ERP] system "deletes" open orders on invoicing).
- To aggregate performance and data for business needs.
- To add new business terms, rules, and logic to data (e.g., rules that do not exist in source systems).

- To establish central reporting and analysis environments.
- To hold documentation of metadata centrally upon collection of data.
- To secure scalability to ensure future handling of increased data volumes.
- To ensure consistency and valid data definitions across business areas and countries (this principle is called *one version of the truth*).
- Overall, a well-planned data warehouse enables the organization to create a qualitative, well-documented, true set of figures with history across source systems and business areas—and as a scalable solution.

ARCHITECTURE AND PROCESSES IN A DATA WAREHOUSE

The architecture and processes in an enterprise data warehouse (EDW) will typically look as illustrated in Exhibit 5.1. The exhibit is the pivot for the rest of this chapter.

As opposed to the approach we've used so far in this book, we will now discuss the data warehouse based on the direction in which data and information actually move (from the bottom up). Our point of departure in previous chapters has been the direction that is dictated by the requirements for information (from the top-down). The bottom-up approach here is chosen for pedagogical reasons and reflects the processes that take place in a data warehouse. This does not, however, change the fact that the purpose of a data warehouse is to collect information required by the organization's business side.

As is shown by the arrows in Exhibit 5.1, the extract, transform, and load (ETL) processes create dynamics and transformation in a data warehouse. We must be able to extract source data into the data warehouse, transform these, merge them, and load them to different locations. These ETL processes are created by an ETL developer.

Extract, transform, and load is a data warehouse process that always includes these actions:

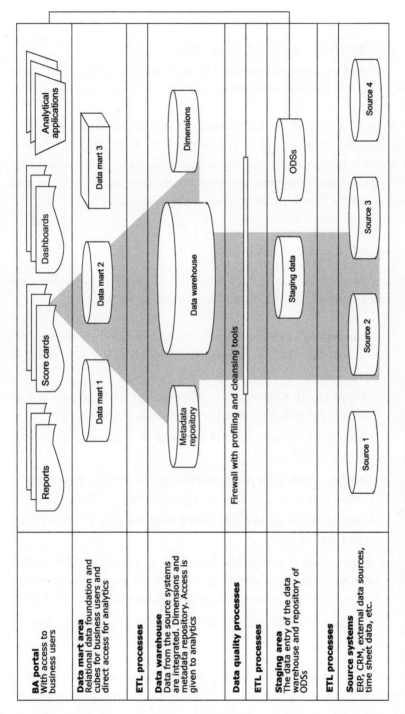

BA portal
With access to business users

Data mart area
Relational data foundation and cubes for business users and direct access for analytics

ETL processes

Data warehouse
Data from the source systems are integrated. Dimensions and metadata repository. Access is given to analytics

Data quality processes

ETL processes

Staging area
The data entry of the data warehouse and repository of ODSs

ETL processes

Source systems
ERP, CRM, external data sources, time sheet data, etc.

Reports Score cards Dashboards Analytical applications

Data mart 1 Data mart 2 Data mart 3

Metadata repository Data warehouse Dimensions

Firewall with profiling and cleansing tools

Staging data ODSs

Source 1 Source 2 Source 3 Source 4

EXHIBIT 5.1 Architecture and Processes in a Data Warehouse

■ **Extract** data from a source table.

■ **Transform** data for business use.

■ **Load** to target table in the data warehouse or different locations outside the data warehouse.

The first part of the ETL process is an extraction from a source table, staging table, or from a table within the actual data warehouse. A series of business rules or functions are used on the extracted data in the transformation phase. In other words, you may need to use one or more of the transformation types in the following section.

Selection of Certain Columns to Be Loaded

It's necessary to choose the columns that should be loaded. Here are the conditions under which columns need to be loaded:

■ **Translating coded values.** If the source system is storing "M" for man and "W" for woman, but the data warehouse wants to store the value 1 for man and 2 for woman.

■ **Mapping of values.** For example, mapping of the values "Man," "M" and "Mr." into the new value 1.

■ **Calculating a new calculated value.** For example, sales = number × unit price.

■ **Joining from different sources.** For example, to look-up or merge.

■ **Summing up of several rows of data.** For example, total sales for all regions.

■ **Generating a surrogate key.** This is a unique value that is attributed to a row or an object in the database. The surrogate key is not in the source system; it is attributed by the ETL tool.

■ **Transposing.** Changing multiple columns to multiple rows or vice versa.

In the load phase of the ETL process, data is entered in the data warehouse or moved from one area of the data warehouse to another.

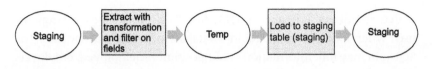

EXHIBIT 5.2 Example of a Simple ETL Job

There is always a target table that is filled with the result of the transformation in the load procedure. Depending on the organization's requirements, this process can vary greatly. For example, in some data warehouses, old data is overwritten by new data. Systems of a certain complexity are able to create data history simply by making "notes" in the data warehouse if a change occurs in the source data (e.g., if a customer has moved to a new address).

Exhibit 5.2 shows a simple ETL job, where data is extracted from the source table (Staging). Then the selected fields are transferred to the temporary table (Temp), which, through the load object, is sent on to the table (Staging) in the staging area. The transformation of the job is simple, since it's just a case of selecting a subset of the columns or fields of the source table. The load procedure of the ETL job may overwrite the old rows in the target table or insert new rows.

A more complex part of an ETL job is shown in Exhibit 5.3. Here data is extracted from three staging tables. Note that only selected columns and rows are extracted with a filter function; an example of this could be rows that are valid for only a certain period. These three temporary tables in the center of Exhibit 5.3 are joined using

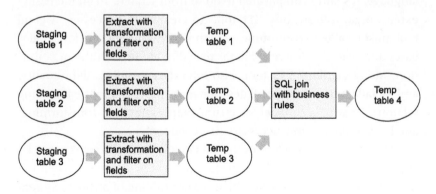

EXHIBIT 5.3 Part of ETL Job with SQL Join

structured query language (SQL). SQL is a programming language used when manipulating data in a database or a data warehouse.) The SQL join may link information about position (unemployed, employee, self-employed, etc.) to information about property evaluations and lending information. There may also be conditions (business rules) that filter out all noncorporate customers. The procedure is a transformation and joining of data, which ends up in the temporary table (Temp Table 4). The table with the joined information about loan applicants (again, Temp Table 4) then flows on in the ETL job with further transformations based on business rules, until it is finally loaded to a target table in the staging area, the actual data warehouse, or for reporting and analytics in a data mart.

When initiating ETL processes and choosing tools, there are certain things to bear in mind, because ETL processes can be very complex, and significant operational problems may arise if the ETL tools are not in order. Further complexity may be a consequence of many source systems with many different updating cycles. Some are updated every minute, and others on a weekly basis. A good ETL tool must be able to withhold certain data until all sources are synchronized.

The degree of scalability in the performance of the ETL tool in its lifetime and use should also be taken into consideration in the analysis phase. This includes an understanding of the volume of data to be processed. The ETL tool may need to be scalable in order to process terabytes of data, if such data volumes are included.

Even though ETL processes can be performed in any programming language, it's fairly complicated to do so from scratch. To an increasing extent, organizations buy ETL tools to create ETL processes. A good tool must be able to communicate with many different relational databases and read the different file formats that are used in the organization. Many vendors' ETL tools also offer data profiling, data quality, and metadata handling (we'll describe these processes in the following section). That is, a broader spectrum than extracting, transforming, and loading data is now necessary in a good tool.

The scope of data values or the data quality in a data source may be reduced, compared with the expectations held by designers when the transformation rules were specified. Data profiling of a source system is recommended to identify the usability of the transformations on all imaginable future data values.

Staging Area and Operational Data Stores

Extract, transform, and load processes transfer business source data from the operational systems (e.g., the accounting system) to a staging area, usually either raw and unprocessed or transformed by means of simple business rules. The staging area is a temporary storing facility in the area before the data warehouse (see Exhibit 5.1). Source systems use different types of formats on databases (e.g., relational databases such as Oracle, DB2, SQL Server, MySQL, SAS, or flat text files). After extraction, data is converted to a format that the ETL tools can subsequently use to transform this data. In the staging area, data is typically arranged as flat files in a simple text format or in the preferred format of the data warehouse, which could be Oracle. Normally, new data extracts or rows will be added to tables in the staging area. The purpose is to accumulate the history of the base systems.

In the staging area, many subsequent complex ETL processes may be performed, which upon completion are scheduled for processing with an operations management tool. The tables may be transformed hundreds of times on several levels before data is ready to leave for the actual data warehouse.

If the business needs to access data with only a few minutes' delay—for example, because the contents are risks calculated on the portfolio values of the bank—it may make sense to implement an operational data store (ODS). This will enable business users to access this data instantly. Typically, it will not be a requirement that data in a data warehouse be accessible for business analyses until the following day, even though the trend of the future is real-time information. Pervasive BA, as we've mentioned earlier, requires real-time data from the data warehouse. The ETL jobs that update rows in a data warehouse and in data marts will usually run overnight, and be ready with fresh data the next morning, when business users arrive for work. In some situations, however, instant access is required, in which case an ODS is needed.

Causes and Effects of Poor Data Quality

Data quality is a result of how complete the data is, whether you've got duplicates, and the level of accuracy and consistency across the overall organization. Most data quality projects have been linked to individual BA or CRM projects. Organizations know that correct data (e.g., complete and accurate customer contact data for CRM) is essential to achieve a positive return on these investments. Therefore, they are beginning to understand the significant advantage that is associated with focusing on data quality at a strategic level.

Data quality is central in all data integration initiatives, too. Data from a data warehouse can't be used in an efficient way until it has been analyzed and cleansed. In terms of data warehouses, it's becoming more and more common to install an actual storage facility or a firewall, which ensures quality when data is loaded from the staging area to the actual data warehouse. To ensure that poor data quality from external sources does not destroy or reduce the quality of internal processes and applications, organizations should establish this data quality firewall in their data warehouse. Analgous to a network firewall, whose objective is to keep hackers, viruses, and other undesirables out of the organization's network, the data quality firewall must keep data of poor quality out of internal processes and applications. The firewall can analyze incoming data as well as cleanse data by means of known patterns of problems, so that data will be of a certain quality, before it arrives in the data warehouse. Poor data that cannot be cleansed will be rejected by the firewall. The proactive way to improve the data quality is to subsequently identify poor data and add new patterns in the cleansing procedures of the firewall or track them back to the perpetrators and communicate the quality problems to the data source owners.

Poor data quality is very costly and can cause breakdowns in the organization's value chains (e.g., no items in stock) and lead to impaired decision making at management and operational levels. Equally, it may lead to substandard customer service, which will cause dissatisfaction and cancellation of business. Lack of trust in reporting is another problem here, which will delay budgeting processes. In other words, poor data quality affects the organization's competiveness negatively.

The first step toward improved data quality in the data warehouse will typically be the deployment of tools for data profiling. By means of advanced software, basic statistical analyses are performed to search for frequencies and column widths on the data in the tables. Based on the statistics, we can see, for example, frequencies on nonexistent or missing postal codes as well as the number of rows without a customer name. Incorrect values of sales figures in transaction tables can be identified by means of analyses of the numeric widths of the columns. Algorithms searching for different ways of spelling the same content are carried out with the purpose of finding customers who appear under several names. For example, "Mr. Thomas D. Marchand" could be the same customer as "ThomasD. Marchand." Is it the same customer twice? Software packages can disclose whether data fits valid patterns and formats. Phone numbers, for instance, must have the format "35-831176" and not "35831176" or "358 3 1176". Data profiling can also identify superfluous data and whether business rules are observed (e. g., whether two fields contain the same data and whether sales and distributions are calculated correctly in the source system). Some programs offer functionality for calculating indicators or KPIs for data quality, which enables the business to follow the development in data quality over time.

Poor data quality may also be a result of the business analytics function introducing new requirements. If a source system is registering only the date of a business transaction (e.g., 12 April 2010), the BA initiative cannot analyze the sales distribution over the hours of the working day. The initiative will not be possible unless the source system is reprogrammed to register business transactions with a time-stamp such as "12APR2010:12:40:31." Data will now show that the transaction took place 40 minutes and 31 seconds past 12, on 12 April 2010. The data quality is now secured, and the BA initiative can be carried out.

Data profiling is thus an analysis of the problems we are facing. In the next phase, the improvement of data quality, the process starts with the development of better data. In other words, this means correcting errors, securing accuracy, and validating and standardizing data with a view to increase their reliability. Based on data profiling, tools introduce intelligent algorithms to cleanse and improve data.

"Fuzzy" merge technology is frequently used here. Using this technology means that duplicate rows can often be removed, so that customers appear only once in the system. Rows without customer names can be removed. Data with incorrect postal codes can be corrected, or removed. Phone numbers are adjusted to the desired format, such as XXX-XXX-XXXX.

Data cleansing is a process that identifies and corrects (or removes) ruined or incorrect rows in a table. After the cleansing, the dataset will be consistent with other datasets elsewhere in the system. Ruined data can be a result of user entries or transmission errors. The actual data cleansing process may involve a comparison between entered values and a known list of possible values. The validation may be "hard," so that all rows without valid postal codes are rejected or deleted, or it can be "soft," which means that values are adjusted if they partly resemble the listed values. As mentioned previously, data quality tools are usually implemented when data is removed from the staging area to the data warehouse. Simply put, data moves through a kind of firewall with cleansing tools. Not all errors, however, can be corrected by the data quality tools. Entry error by users can be difficult to identify, but some of them will come through in the data profiling as very high or low values. Missing data caused by fields that have not been filled in should be corrected by means of validation procedures in the source system. (For details, see Chapter 6.) It should not be optional, for instance, whether the business user in sales selects one individual customer or not.

The Data Warehouse: Functions, Components, and Examples

In the actual data warehouse, the processed and merged figures from the source systems are presented (e.g., transactions, inventory, and master data). A modern data warehouse typically works as a storage area for the organization's dimensions as well as a metadata repository. First, we'll look at the dimensions of the business, and then we'll explain the concept of the metadata repository.

From the staging area, the data sources are collected, joined, and transformed in the actual data warehouse. One of the most important processes is that the business's transactions (facts) are then enriched with dimensions such as organizational relationship, and placement in the product hierarchy, before data is sent on to the data mart area. This will then enable analysts and business users to prepare interactive reports via "slice and dice" (i.e., to break down figures into their components) techniques. As a starting point, a business transaction has no dimensions when it arrives in the data warehouse from the staging area. That means that we cannot answer questions about when, where, who, what, or why. A business transaction is merely a fact or an event, which in itself is completely useless for reporting and analysis purposes.

An example of a meaningless statement for an analyst is "Our sales were $25.5 million." The business will typically want answers to questions about when, for what, where, by whom, for whom, in which currency? And dimensions are exactly what enable business users or the analyst to answer the following questions:

- **When did it happen?** Which year, quarter, month, week, day, time?
- **Where and to whom did it happen?** Which salesperson, which department, which business area, which country?
- **What happened?** What did we make on which product and on which product group?

All these questions are relevant to the analyst.

Dimensional modeling is a popular way of organizing data in a data warehouse for analysis and reporting—and not without reason. The starting point is the previously listed transactions or facts. It may also be helpful to look at the organization's facts as events. These fact rows are enriched with dimensions in a data warehouse to provide perspective.

The dimensions in Exhibit 5.4 surrounding the facts or transactions put the sales figures, revenue figures, and cost figures into a perspective. This type of illustration is also called a *star schema*. Among other things, it gives business users and analysts the opportunity to get answers from the data warehouse such as these: "Our sales in product

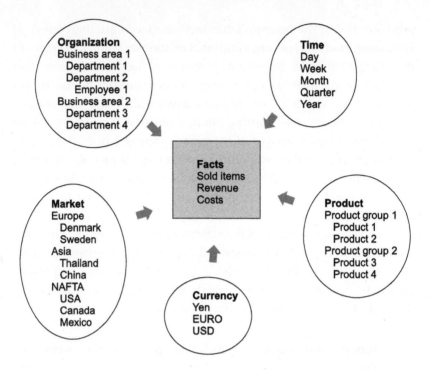

EXHIBIT 5.4 Fact-Based Transactions Surrounded by Multidimensional Perspectives

group 1 in December in the USA, measured in the currency USD, were 2 million," and these: "Sales in department 2 of business area 1 in the first quarter in Europe, measured in the currency Euro, were 800,000." Note that the dimensions answer questions about when, for what, where, for whom, and by whom. Business reality is viewed multidimensionally to create optimum insight. Generally speaking, the multidimensional perspective enables the business to answer the question: "Why did things turn out as they did?"

Note the hierarchies in the dimensions in Exhibit 5.4. The organization consists, for instance, of a number of business areas. Under each of these areas, we've got a number of departments, and in each department, we've got a number of employees. The hierarchies provide us with the opportunity to "slice and dice." A sales figure for the overall organization can be broken down into business areas. Each business area can then be broken down into departments, and the department figures can be broken down into individual employees. Note that these features are especially helpful when the business—on a daily basis—is analyzing information by itself and is therefore not drawing on quantitative analyst resources.

A modern data warehouse will normally contain a metadata repository. Here information is stored about business data. The simplest definition of metadata is *data about data*. Metadata facilitates the understanding of data with a view to using and managing data. Metadata has been given a central role as businesses are becoming increasingly demanding of documentation. In relation to a camera, where data is a digital photo, metadata will typically contain information about the date the photo was taken, the settings of the camera, name of manufacturer, size, and resolution. Libraries have registered metadata about books to facilitate searches. This metadata includes title, genre, publishing year, author of the book, and so forth. Without metadata, it would be difficult or almost impossible to find the relevant data (books).

The documentation of data and tables is of equal importance, and the demands for metadata registration in the data warehouse have grown considerably in recent years. Previously, it was sufficient if tables and fields had meaningful names. The simplest way to create metadata about tables and fields is to give these meaningful names. For instance, consider a revenue table containing the two fields Revenue and Time. That should make it obvious what the table contains! The problem is, however, that other users than the ones who made the table might interpret the contents of the revenue field differently. Is it revenue with or without value-added tax (VAT)? Are discounts included in the figures? Is the revenue figure in USD or Euro? And those are just a few different interpretation possibilities.

Understandably, the previous metadata registration is no longer sufficient. A better metadata registration can be performed using labels on the fields of the tables. The revenue field could have a label explaining the contents precisely: revenue excluding VAT including discounts in USD. That would increase the quality of the metadata, and data could be used by other users. But we still have the problem that users must be able to search through tables for fields with, for instance, revenue contents (just like when we search for books at the library).

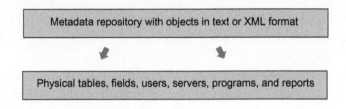

EXHIBIT 5.5   The Metadata Repository

Many BA vendors have taken action on the consequence of customers' need for advanced metadata registration and search options for the average user. They have created one single metadata layer in text format (XML format, in fact), that points to physical tables, fields, users, servers, programs, and reports. This layer can be found in the metadata repository of the data warehouse. (See Exhibit 5.5.)

The metadata repository has become one of the BA vendors most important upgrading and sales arguments. And the arguments are compelling. The metadata layer produces documentation about everything that goes on in the data warehouse and the front-end portal. Some software developers are working along the lines that reports cannot be produced if they are not registered in the metadata repository of the data warehouse. Similarly, a physical table is not available to the reporting environment without metadata registration. The same situation occurs with users, servers, and so on. A metadata repository has become key, since all Web inquiries must go through the metadata layer via the metadata server. This results in visibility and documentation of everything that goes on, and this is considered of increasing importance to the business. These days, it's almost unthinkable to build a data warehouse structure without a central metadata repository. In the top layer of the BA platform, where users access reports and data, this metadata repository also enables users to search on data definitions and reports from the Web interface, as if they were books at the library.

The users of Apple's iTunes software know about metadata registration in XML format. An XML file in your iTunes library on your personal computer contains all the information about tracks, albums, and artists, and so forth. iTunes uses this vital file to navigate. If you copy one MP3 music file with Microsoft Explorer to your physical music library outside of iTunes, it won't appear in your iTunes music collection, and you won't be able to search for it or play it, because information about the existence of the file and other data is not metadata that is registered via your iTunes software.

Data marts for the support of business processes are the end products delivered by the data warehouse and thus contain information for business users. A data mart is a specialized version of a data warehouse. Like a data warehouse, a data mart is a snapshot of operational data to help business users make decisions or make strategic analyses (e.g., based on historical trends). The difference between a data mart and a data warehouse is that data marts are created based on the particular reporting needs of specific and well-defined user groups, and data marts provide easy business access to relevant information. A data mart is thus designed to answer the users' specific questions. Relevant dimensions for the business area have been linked to data, and specific business rules apply to help users move about in the desired dimensions and hierarchies. An organization may have several data marts for different functions, such as marketing, sales, finance, human resources, and others. A data mart is normally structured as a dimensional model such as a star schema and made up of fact tables and dimension tables and using specific business rules. An online analytical processing (OLAP) cube or a pivot table is a way of arranging data in areas (arrays) to facilitate quick data analyses, and it is often used for data marts. The arrays are called cubes.)

An organization may have many data marts, each of which might be relevant to one or more business units that they have been designed for. Many business units have assumed "ownership" of their data marts, and this includes hardware, software, and data. This ownership enables each business unit or department or business area to use, manipulate, and develop their data to suit their needs, without changing any information in other data marts or centrally in the data warehouse.

Another reason for gathering data in small marts is that time is saved in connection with queries, simply because there is less data to process. This means, too, that two different data marts may present exactly the same information, except that one presents it in much

EXHIBIT 5.6 A Book Seller's Sales Table

ID	ISBN	Title	Type	Date	Number	Price
1	1234	Peter Pan	Paperback	23-10-2010	1	59.00
2	5678	The Hobbit	Hardback	24-10-2010	1	159.00
3	9101	Moby Dick	Paperback	25-10-2010	2	79.00

more detail, which can then be used if the user decides he or she needs detailed information.

When data has been joined and enriched with dimensions in the data warehouse, data can be extracted for business use to data marts. These ETL processes will use many different business rules according to individual user needs. A data mart may cover the accounting function's need for a consolidated set of figures with the specific business rules required. Another data mart may cover the need for performance monitoring of the organization's sales processes.

As stated previously, the database for data marts may be relational or OLAP cubes. The functional difference between these two types of data is of great significance to analysts and business users, among other reasons because the difference affects response times and analytical scope. A relational data model is a model where data is organized using common characteristics. The order of the rows doesn't matter; only the number of rows is important because the number affects how quickly extracts can be performed. The order of the columns is of no importance, either. Transaction-based tables are always relational as explained in the following section.

The sales table in Exhibit 5.6 has seven columns and three rows, and is a simple example of what a relational transaction table looks like. In this kind of table, we can quickly add a new transaction from the shop, when another item is sold.

For adding, processing, and extracting data from relational tables, we use the programming language SQL, which is a formalized way of talking to databases. If we want to know the book shop's revenue distributed on the types "paperback" and "hardback," we can send the following SQL syntax off to the database:

EXHIBIT 5.7 A Book Shop's Revenue

Type	Revenue
Hardback	159.00
Paperback	217.00

```
Create Table REVENUE as
Select TYPE, SUM (NUMBER * PRICE) as REVENUE
From Sales_Table
Group by TYPE
Order by TYPE
```

We will then receive a revenue dataset that looks like Exhibit 5.7.

Large enterprises, such as WalMart, have several hundred million transactions a year, and it doesn't take a lot of imagination to see that response times in reporting can be very long if a preceding summary of the relational tables is not carried out, or if a reporting mart with a database in the shape of an OLAP cube is not created.

Once the OLAP cube is created, you can't just add another row as with relational tables. By using this way of arranging data in cubes, we avoid the limitation of relational databases, as these are not suitable for instant (real-time) analysis of large data volumes. The relational database is more suited for creating rows in a table of a series of transactions. Even though many reporting tools are developed for relational data, these are slow when it comes to summing up large databases. In an OLAP cube, all summing up and calculating are carried out beforehand; we just pull out a value from the cube, so to speak, and we therefore do not need to sum up something like a million rows in the extract.

In the OLAP cube in Exhibit 5.8, each little subcube contains a sales figure that is calculated beforehand for the different sets of

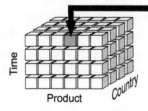

Sale of coats in Denmark in July

EXHIBIT 5.8 OLAP Cube with Sales Figures and Three Dimensions or Perspectives

dimensional values. The sale of a certain product (coats) in a certain country (Denmark) within a certain period (the month of July) could be the little dark cube in Exhibit 5.8. The clever thing about the OLAP cube is that when the business user requests information about the sales of coats in Denmark in July, all the involved transactions do not need to be summed up. Instead the extract application runs straight into the cube via some index values, and extracts just one single pre-calculated summed-up figure, which is then returned to the user's client software.

The OLAP cube can be seen as an expansion of a two-dimensional spreadsheet. A controller (financial analyst) will need to analyze financial data by product, by period of time, by town, type of revenue, or cost and then compare actuals with budget figures. Each of these dimensions may have in-built hierarchies. The controller will begin at a summarized level (such as the total difference between actual revenue and budgeted revenue), and then perform a "drill down" or "slice and dice" in the cube to discover entities, products, sales people, or periods of time that are accountable for the difference in the total figures.

Note that the size of an OLAP cube increases exponentially with the adding of more dimensions to the cube or when the number of categories in individual dimensions grow, which naturally affects performance and response times.

Business Analytics Portal: Functions and Examples

Business analytics tools and portals aim to deliver information to operational decision makers. In most cases, this information comes from relational databases and OLAP cubes in the organization's data warehouse, and the information is presented to business users as scorecards, dashboards, conventional retrospective sales reports, business performance management (BPM) dashboards, and analytical applications. End users access the BA portal on top of the organization's data warehouse (see Exhibit 5.1). The BA portal constitutes a small part of the overall process to deliver BA decision support for the business. A rule of thumb is that the portal part constitutes only 15% of the work, while 85% of the work lies in the data collection and processing in the data warehouse.

In the past, BA tools have been developed from individual applications to serve as critical plug-ins in the organization's global portals. The requirements for vendors of BA portals are therefore now focused on their ability to completely integrate all kinds of BA tools into one global portal, which then contains all relevant information for decision makers, whether it be employees, partners, customers, or vendors.

Developments are moving quickly toward global BA portals, and the key to a successful implementation of such a portal that completely integrates BA tools is to acknowledge that the portal is not just the launching pad for applications. The portal must deliver true business value and allow users access to business critical information in a dynamic and secure way. Further, the information must be available via different online and mobile units, all of which must be easy for end users to operate.

In the pages that follow, we'll provide examples of user-friendly BA front-ends and dashboards, which can be accessed on a modern BA portal like the SAS Information Delivery Portal. In Exhibit 5.9, we

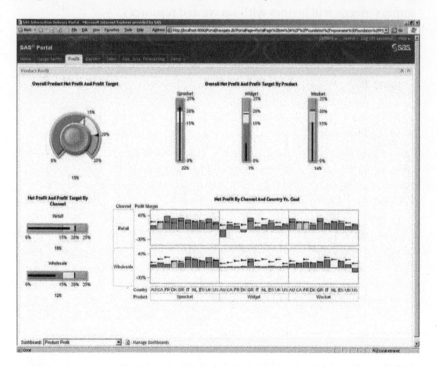

EXHIBIT 5.9 Business Performance Dashboard for KPI Monitoring

see a dashboard with graphics for the monitoring of the performance of product groups.

This BPM dashboard generated by the SAS Enterprise BI Server enables business users to follow product performance (actual profits vs. budget profits) on a monthly or quarterly basis, totaled, distributed on different product groups, channels, and the geographical markets where they are sold. The information in the dashboard is lag information by nature, but users can with simple projections based on trends and colors form an opinion about needs for future performance improvements. In this way, the information can move business processes forward, too (lead information). We then get an answer to the question: "What do we need to do tomorrow?"

Exhibit 5.10 shows a chart produced with SAS/ETS software. The software provides forecasts of demand for services so that organizations can maximize staff resources. It can automatically account for seasonal fluctuations and trends, and can select the best method for generating the demand forecasts. Efficient staff allocations mean customers' needs will be met with no wasted resources.

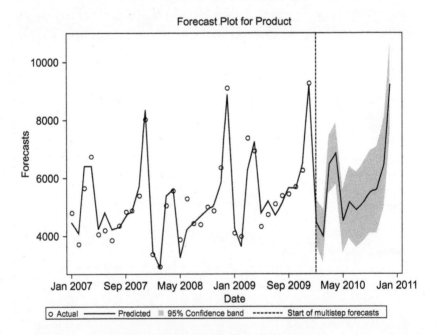

EXHIBIT 5.10   An Example of Forecasting with SAS/ETS Software

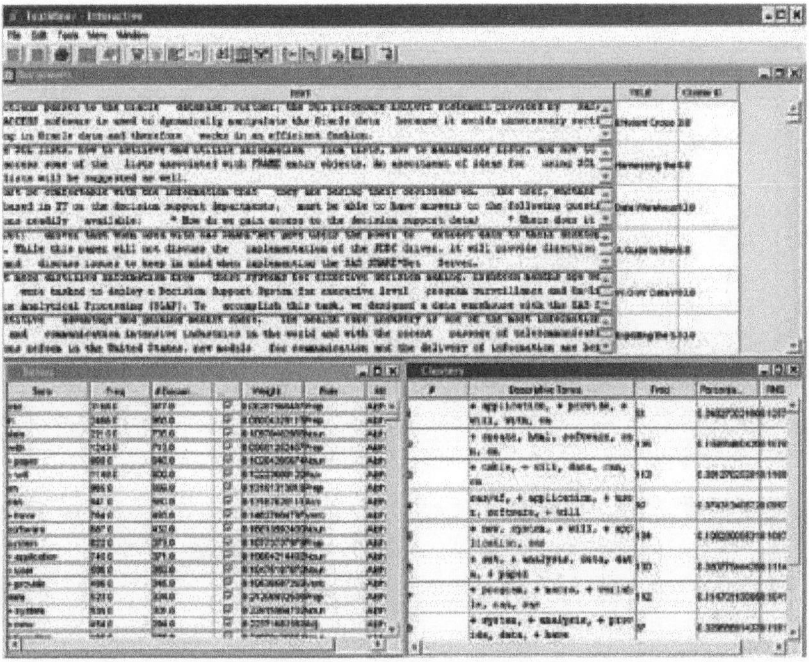

EXHIBIT 5.11 Screenshot of SAS Text Miner

The software package includes both prebuilt and customized reports, allowing you to gain the most from your data. Built-in analysis allows you to understand how visitors navigate your Web site and how they flow through a user-defined set of pages. In addition to showing the drop-off at each step, the reports track users as they flow into, out of, and through the funnel. The report captures where visitors enter the funnel and where they go once they exit. Expandable and collapsible lists of pages show the most popular customer paths.

With text mining analytics, you can classify documents into predefined or data-driven categories, find explicit relationships or associations between documents, and incorporate textual data with structured inputs. (See Exhibit 5.11.) The dynamic exploration component helps you discover patterns in large document collections and allows you to combine those insights with your predictive analytics to gain maximum value from all of your information. By using text mining analytics, world leaders such as Netanyahu and Obama can find out what's being said about them in forums and lists and twitters and

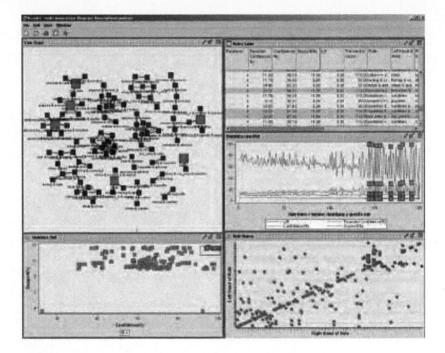

EXHIBIT 5.12   Data Mining Software Identifying Market Basket Profiles

magazine articles and newspapers—in real time—and can have it all boiled down and analyzed.

To gain an edge in today's competitive market, powerful advanced analytic solutions are required to extract knowledge from vast stores of data and act on it. More and more organizations are turning to predictive analytics and data mining software to uncover patterns in data and discover hidden relationships. In Exhibit 5.12, the screenshot from SAS Enterprise Miner lets you identify market basket profiles. You can also interactively subset the rules based on lift, confidence, and support chain length.

TIPS AND TECHNIQUES IN DATA WAREHOUSING

Master Data Management

Problems concerning data quality often lead to discussions about master data management (MDM). When the complexity of the business increases, and the data volumes explode, the business turns toward MDM as an intelligent way of consolidating and managing data. Master data management provides a unified view of data, when data is integrated from different data sources. In organizations that have been growing for a long time, the different business areas will typically have developed different master data concerning customers, transactions, and products. The same applies to merging companies. The need for identical definitions will arise across business areas, national borders, and/or merging companies. For instance, the definition can include what precisely a customer is and which customer data is registered. Using MDM, the business can consolidate these sources to a master reference file, which then feeds information back to the applications. Accuracy and consistency are thus secured across the entire organization.

Service-Oriented Architecture

Service-oriented architecture is a way of thinking about how to use the organization's resources based on a service approach and with the objective of providing a more efficient achievement of overall business targets. It is therefore not a product that you can buy, but rather a design philosophy about how to structure a solution. Service-oriented architecture entails integration across systems. Each IT resource, whether it's an application, a system, or a database, can be reached via a service device. This service function is available via interfaces. Web services are an implementation form that uses specific standards and protocols, when it is executed as an SOA solution.

Service-oriented architecture makes systems more flexible in terms of business needs, simpler to develop further, and easier to maintain and manage. Implementing solutions with a service-oriented architecture facilitates the organization's planning for the future—including when changes occur—and helps it to respond proactively rather than reactively.

What specifically constitutes a service? A service is a program with which the user can interact through well-defined standards for the exchange of messages. Services must be designed for stability and accessibility. There is no point in "making SOA for the sake of SOA."

Service-oriented architecture is undertaken to support the needs of the business. It is especially suitable for organizations that make data and applications available to a large number of customers. An enterprise like wheater.com makes their services available to many customers via SOA. When customers draw on these enterprises' services, they do so via Web interfaces and stable programs that are always available. Communication between systems takes place via well-defined standards/protocols for the exchange of data. Instead of each customer developing various extracts from the wheater.com databases, wheater.com places an application at the customer's disposal that serves the client with data, when a well-defined set of parameters is received in the right protocol format.

In relation to our data warehouse model in Exhibit 5.1, SOA will be represented as interfaces from source systems inwards pointing to the staging area or interfaces from data marts toward users' applications via the BA platform. In addition to making data easily accessible, they must obviously be easily understandable, so users are given outlines of, say, temperature and maps, and not just meteorological terminology and map coordinates from the easily accessible applications.

How Should You Access Your Data?

In this chapter, we have looked at the typical ingredients in a data warehouse solution, from source data to the front-end solution. If we now look at a data warehouse solution in relation to the different information domains that were introduced in Chapter 4, there are some correlations worth mentioning. There are two types of direct users of a data warehouse: the business user and the BA analyst. Since the BA analyst will always make his or her analyses based on business needs, the business user will always be the end user.

When the business user approaches a BA analyst for assistance in accessing the data warehouse, he or she may have two reasons for this. Either the business user is not merely looking for information, or he or she is also looking for an analyst to enrich and interpret this information—that is, to deliver information to the business. This naturally means that the analyst must have business insight, as explained in Chapter 4.

The other reason for a business user to draw on analytical resources is that he or she does not have access to the desired data and is looking for information. As illustrated in Exhibit 5.13, the analyst often has many points of access to the data warehouse. The reason is not that the analyst needs to know more than the rest of the business, but rather that a data warehouse is a dynamic entity that continually adapts to the needs of the business. And since it may take some time for the business to acknowledge and formulate a new need for information, and for the required information to be delivered as standard reports, there will be an implementation period where the analyst will be delivering the required information as manual reports.

Access to BA Portals

Analysts don't actually need access to BA portals because, if they have direct access to the data they are retrieving, they can access the data via their analytical programs. When someone from the business side then requests a report, the analyst can refer to the data managers in the section of the data warehouse that is responsible for the development of reports. In smaller organizations, however, the roles of data managers and analysts will typically be performed by the same person, which means that already here we are starting to see that it doesn't make sense to separate the two roles. There are many other good reasons, however, why analysts, on an equal footing with business users, should have access to and be keen users of front-end solutions.

Analysts will often make considerable use of BA portals because they provide fast and easy access to data. Obviously, analysts are not using this data in connection with the continual development of manual reports, because if there is a front-end access to the required information, the end user can retrieve them there themselves. An analyst will typically use a BA portal in connection with the development of new reports, score cards, or dashboards, in cases where any of these are deemed too complex for the end user to develop. After completed development, they are delivered to end users, who can then continually update the contents of the reports, when new data is entered into the data mart, or on request.

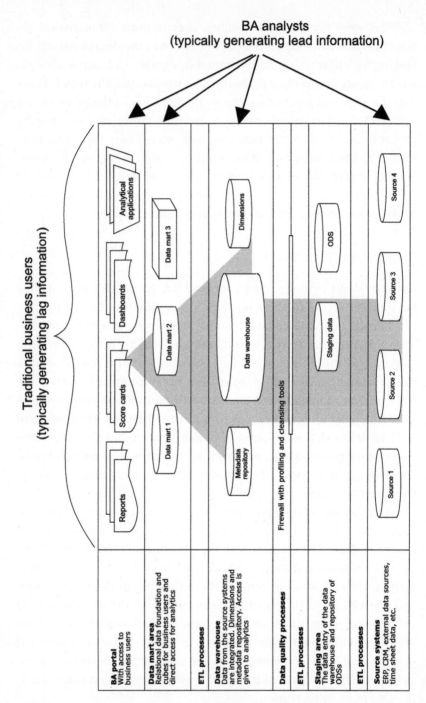

EXHIBIT 5.13 The BA Analyst's Various Accesses to the Data Warehouse

Analysts use front-end solutions, too, in connection with the validation of data drawn directly from the data warehouse. If an analysis is based on a linkage of five different extracts collected by means of SQL directly from the data warehouse, there will typically be hundreds of lines of programming to validate. This will, of course, not be a case of a one-to-one validation, because then the analyst would have used the front-end solutions only. But it may be in connection with segmentations based on information that is available only from the data warehouse and not from the data marts, where we, for instance, want to validate that we have included all customers in our analysis. We therefore want to compare the number of segmented customers with the official number of customers. And if these two figures are not the same, we have an error in our segmentation. Since analysts also frequently have a high degree of contact with the people who make decisions based on data warehouse information, analysts must train their end users in the functionality offered by the BA portal.

Access to Data Mart Areas

It is tempting to argue that analysts do not need direct access to retrieve data from data marts, if they already have access to data via BA portals. The thinking here is that it is possible to transfer data to the front-end and save it as a flat file, which can then be transferred to a statistics or data mining program. However, several arguments are against this: First, it's important to be able to automate processes, which is the opposite of manual processes where the analyst retrieves, saves, and imports data via physical routines. Second, in connection with data mining solutions, where the same data must be presented in the same way month after month, there are great savings to be had in automating such processes. It therefore becomes a question of what the analyst should be spending his or her time on: moving data around or analyzing it.

Some front-ends pose problems in terms of being able to collect only a certain number of rows at a time or having the user be timed out after a short period, which is not the case with analytical programs. Their limitation is the hardware and the bandwidth. Direct access to data marts can therefore ensure that all rows are included. Another argument for analysts to have access to both front-end solutions and data marts is that a front-end can function as an SQL generator. If our analysts' expertise is not precisely the development of SQL, SQL requests can be generated in the front-end solution and copied and pasted into a statistics program, which can also use the access of the front-end solution to the data mart. In this way, we can automate data delivery via open database connectivity (ODBC) entries and ensure that our analysts stay focused on analytics, which is difficult enough. In connection with data mining projects, where data access can be a considerable consumer of time, this specifically means that the data access can be carried out faster, if we focus solely on easily accessible information from our data marts. Once our data mining processes are up and running, we can then start to collect more raw information directly from the data warehouse. Moreover, this approach supports what is generally recommended when establishing BA projects, which is: "Think big, start small, and deliver fast."

Access to Data Warehouse Areas

Having access to these areas enables analysts to provide the business with answers that they may otherwise not get, via front-end solutions. The reason that only analysts can access some data is not a question about withholding information in data. It's a question of establishing front-end solutions that present information in the most accessible way possible based on users' needs and the skills of the business users in general.

A supermarket, for example, may be reporting on revenue from different products, summarizing products into categories, such as milk and butter. But since it would be too difficult for the user to get an overview or it would take up too much space in the data mart, we can choose to omit information about which particular milk or butter brand. If we want this information, we'll have to drill right down into the data warehouse.

There are several reasons why a business wants answers to questions that cannot be clarified via the BA portal. Needs may change over time, questions may arise in connection with ad hoc tasks that do not require regular reporting, and a business may want to implement complex analytical solutions. Data mining could be such a case, where the person driving the solution is called a data miner, and not a typical business user. Data mining is generally associated with a business looking to use information as a strategic resource, not because the analytical method as such can justify this, but because it is a strategic decision that forms the basis of the investment in this competence area. As a result, data mining projects of a certain complexity depend on the data miner or analyst working with direct access to the data warehouse. Furthermore, the results of the data mining process (segmentations and recommended actions in relation to customers) will usually be distributed via the data warehouse to the CRM systems whose users are typically acting on the data mining information.

Access to Source Systems

Access to source systems is something analysts do not always have if a data warehouse has already been established. This access is usually not automated, which is the reason why people often associate considerable time consumption with the use of information obtained directly from source systems. In addition to this, data quality can be quite variable, depending on what the information is used for in the source system. And also the source system itself might suffer in performance if accessed as a data warehouse. Developments in these cases will be that if information of significant value is identified in the source systems, a process will be started to ensure that this information becomes accessible in the data warehouse. If the business does not have a data warehouse, analysts always work directly with source systems, in spite of the weaknesses this entails. Over time, an analyst will usually want to carry out regular runs every month for reporting; the dataset generated here can therefore be seen as a data warehouse at the simplest level, and as a quantity to be optimized.

In recent years, companies have come to realize the strengths and weaknesses of the Internet. There has been a growing understanding of the fact that, for instance, customer behavior on a company's Web site is relevant CRM information, too. It is not without relevance, for instance, for a telecom company to know whether a given customer has checked the company's Web site to find out how to cancel his or her subscription. If this information is then combined with information about the customer's value as well, it can be decided whether a "loyalty call" should be made to the customer in question. Long term, the company could structure its Internet portals so that the users' way of moving around these portals will affect the way this customer is treated. The Web site thereby becomes a questionnaire completed by the customer via his or her clicking, instead of merely providing information and automated services.

Generally speaking, though, Web log files are not yet providing the company with information about how customers and users use Web portals. In connection with commercials, however, there are exceptions such as Amazon.com and a few search engines that are related to commercials that specifically and successfully use Web information as a strategic resource that can provide them with a competitive advantage. In these extreme cases, it seems possible to collect and use information to drive the company's strategy.

SUMMARY

In this chapter, we have discussed how to store data to best support business processes and thereby the request for value creation. We also looked into the architecture and processes in a data warehouse.

Business analytics is not possible without access to a combined data foundation from the organization's data-creating source systems. In fact, that is exactly what a data warehouse does, as it increases the usability and availability of source data, as will be explored further in Chapter 6.

One central enterprise data warehouse ensures consistent, integrated, and valid data definitions across business areas and countries. This principle of *one version of the truth* is fundamental for companies to avoid spending much time with contradictory reports and deviating business plans (budgets).

The Company's Collection of Source Data

Source data for business analytics is created by the company's operational systems—accounts entries are, for instance, created in the financial management system and sales data (order data) is created through order pages on the company's Web site. It is here that data quality is of the utmost importance, because this is where data is created.

This chapter will answer the question: How does a business collect source data? We will go through typical data-generating systems in the business's immediate environment, and we'll also look at the difference between primary and secondary data, as well as external and internal analyses. We'll be looking at initiatives to improve the data quality of source systems. Finally, we'll present a way in which a business can prioritize from which source systems to collect project-related data.

An interesting observation is that primary data from source systems meets an information need for a particular target group in the business. When the same data then becomes secondary data in the data warehouse framework, it meets a *different* information need for a *different* target group.

This chapter—and the concept of source data—might seem less relevant than the topics of the previous chapters as a topic for this book. However, consider that you are about to use information as a strategic innovative asset. This means that you should know your strategy in terms of which competitive advantages you want to gain in the long run and which issues you want to overcome in the short run. You should also know which potential improved operational procedures and improved decision support all your potential data sources can give you. When you link future and present business needs with potential and present data sources, you are able to see information as a strategic asset and lead your business with confidence into the future. The point is that strategies do not come out of nowhere. They are based on planning processes that are no better than the planners. If planners do not see the potential in source data, they cannot create strategies that take information into account. If your organization is headed by those who are outdated in their thinking, those who are relying on the same old tricks as the industrial winners back in the 1990s, consider this: Can they carry your organization through the analytical age to come?

WHAT ARE SOURCE SYSTEMS, AND WHAT CAN THEY BE USED FOR?

Source systems is not a general term to be used for some systems and not others. When we use the term *source systems*, our starting point is a given data warehouse, where source systems are the data sources on which the data warehouse is based. Many companies have several data warehouses that are more or less integrated in order that these data warehouses can function as source systems to each other, too.

When we talk about *data-generating systems*, we can, however, specify which systems create data for the first time, and which don't. A checkout register is, for example, a data-generating system, because when it is scanning products, it is also generating data files, and these files in turn tell the store which products at which time and at which price are leaving the store. When the day is over, the customer has gone home, and the register is balanced, the store can choose to delete the data in the register—but we don't always want to do that because this data can be used for many other things. When we choose to save the information, the data-generating system becomes a source system for one or several specific data warehouses. Based on this data warehouse information, we can carry out a large number of analyses and business initiatives (e.g., inventory management, supply chain management, earnings analyses, multipurchase analyses, etc.).

New data is, in other words, not generated in a data warehouse. Data in a data warehouse comes from somewhere else, and is saved based on business rules and generated to meet the company's information requirements. Just as in the previous chapter, we have listed a number of source systems to give an impression of what source systems might be and how they can create value. Keep in mind that neither the list of source systems nor their value-creating potential is exhaustive. Chapter 7, which looks at the organization of business intelligence competency centers, will provide more inspiration through ways in which to achieve strategic influence.

Some examples of data-generating source systems are:

- **Billing systems.** These systems print bills to named customers. By analyzing this data, we can carry out behavior-based segmentations, value-based segmentations, etc.

- **Reminder systems.** These systems send out reminders to customers who do not settle their bills on time. By analyzing this data, we can carry out credit scoring and treat our customers based on their payment records.

- **Debt collection systems.** These systems send statuses on cases that have been transferred to external debt collectors. This data provides the information about which customers we do not wish to have any further dealings with, and which should therefore be removed from customer relationship management (CRM) campaigns, until a settlement is reached.

- **CRM systems.** These systems contain history about customer calls and conversations. This is key information about customers, which can provide input for analyses of complaint behavior and thus what the organization must do better. It can also provide information about which customers draw considerably on service resources and therefore represent less value. It is input for the optimization of customer management processes (see "Optimizing Existing Business Processes" in Chapter 3). It's used in connection with analyses of which customers have left and why.

- **Product and consumption information.** This information can tell us something about which products and services are sold out over time. If we can put a name to individual customers, this information will closely resemble billing information, only without amounts. Even if we are unable to put a name to this information, it will still be valuable for multipurchase analyses, as explained in "The Product and Innovation Perspective" in Chapter 2.

- **Customer information.** These are names, addresses, entry time, any cancellations, special contracts, segmentations, and so forth. This is basic information about our customers, for which we want to collect all market information. This point was explained in the customer relations perspective in Chapter 3.

- **Business information.** This is information such as industry codes, number of employees, or accounting figures. It is identical to customer information for companies operating in the business-to-business (B2B) market. This information can be purchased from a large number of data suppliers, such as Dun & Bradstreet. It is often used to set up sales calls.

- **Campaign history.** Specifically, who received which campaigns when? This is essential information for marketing functions, since this information enables follow-up on the efficiency of marketing initiatives. If our campaigns are targeted toward named customers, and we subsequently are able to see which customers change behavior after a given campaign, we are able to monitor our campaigns closely. If our campaigns are launched via mass media, we can measure effect and generate learning through statistical forecasting models. If this information is aggregated over more campaigns, we will learn which campaign elements are critical and we will learn about overall market development as well.

■ **Web logs.** This is information about user behavior on the company's Web site. It can be used as a starting point to disclose the number of visitors and their way of navigating around the Web site. If the user is also logged in or accepts cookies, we can begin to analyze the development of the use of the Web site. If the customer has bought something from us, it constitutes CRM information in line with billing information.

■ **Questionnaire analyses performed over time.** If we have named users, this will be CRM information that our customers may also expect us to act on. Questionnaire surveys can be a two-edged sword, however; if we ask our customers for feedback on our service functions, for instance, they will give us just that, expecting us to then adjust our services to their needs.

■ **Human resources information about employees, their competencies, salaries, history, and so on.** This information is to be used for the optimization of the people side of the organization. It can also be used to disclose who has many absences due to illness and why. Which employees are proven difficult to retain? Which employees can be associated with success as evaluated by their managers? This information is generally highly underrated in large organizations, and public enterprises in particular, which we will substantiate by pointing out that all organizations have this information and that the scarce resource for many organizations is their employees. Similarly, hour registration information can be considered human resources-related information. When hour registration information (consumption of resources) is combined with output information from, for instance, the enterprise resource planning (ERP) system, we can develop a number of productivity key performance indicators (KPIs).

■ **Production information.** This kind of information can be used to optimize production processes, stock control, procurement, and so on. It is central to production companies competing on operational excellence, as described in Chapter 2.

■ **Accumulation of KPIs.** These are used for monitoring processes in the present, but can later be used for the optimization of processes, since they reveal the correlations between activities and the resulting financial performance.

■ **Data mining results.** These results, which may be segmentations, added sales models, or loyalty segmentation, provide history when placed in a data warehouse. Just as with KPIs, this information can be used to create learning about causal relations across several campaigns and thus highlight market mechanisms in a broader context.

■ **Information from ERP systems.** This information includes accounting management systems in which entries are made about the organization's financial transactions for the use of accounting formats. It can be related to KPI information, if we want to disclose correlations between initiatives, and whether results were as expected.

WHICH INFORMATION IS BEST TO USE FOR WHICH TASK?

Now that you have the source information, the question now becomes: How do you use which information? An efficient way of solving this problem is to list all data from generating and storing systems that may contain information that could potentially create value for the project at hand. Then each individual data source is assessed by the following two dimensions:

1. How useful is the information?
2. How accessible is the information?

Sometimes we may find ourselves in situations where we decide to disregard relevant information if this information is too difficult to access. Similarly, we may have easily accessible information with only a marginal relevance to the task at hand. This way of prioritizing information is, for instance, used in data mining, particularly in connection with customer information, which may come from countless sources. For example: Say that we want to create a profile on a monthly basis of customers who leave us or cancel their subscriptions. Based on this profile, we wish to show who is in the high-risk group of canceling next month, and seek to retain these customers. In this case, call lists must be ready within, say, 40 days. This also means—due to time considerations alone—that all the data from the data-generating source systems can't be part of the analyses, and we therefore have to prioritize.

In Exhibit 6.1 we have placed the data sources that we choose to use in connection with the project in the gray area. We therefore have a clear overview of which data sources we have selected and which we have discarded. But the model gives cause for further deliberations. If, in the course of the project, we find that we have time to include additional data sources—or if we find that we are running out of time—the model can help us prioritize.

The model also tells us how the project can be expected to develop over time in terms of data sources. It's worth repeating that in connection with BA projects we should "think big, start small, and deliver fast." This model enables us to maintain the general overview while delivering fast. The general overview, however, could also include some deliberations about whether the business should include, for example, Web logs in its data warehouse in the future. Web logs

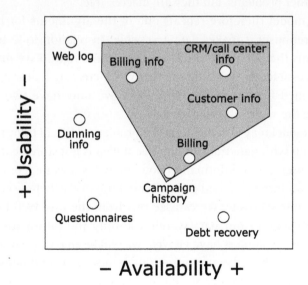

EXHIBIT 6.1 Model for the Prioritization of Data Sources in Connection with Specific BA Projects

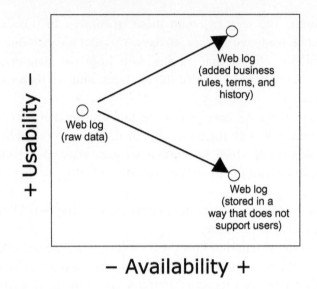

EXHIBIT 6.2 Loss of Information through Transformations

contain useful information in relation to the given problem and maybe also to other problems, but they are inaccessible.

The model therefore repeats one of the arguments for having a data warehouse: It makes data accessible. In relation to Exhibit 6.2, this means that we move the circle toward the right if we make data more accessible. Or we could say that we're creating a new circle that is positioned further to the right, since we now have two ways of accessing the same information.

The model may also highlight the problem of loss of information in connection with data transformations. If data is not stored correctly in terms of user needs, information potentially loses value. For example, if we are an Internet-based company wishing to clarify how customers navigate our Web site, we can see this from the raw Web log. If we choose to save in our data warehouse only the information about which pages customers have viewed, we will be able to see only where the customers have been, not how they moved around between the pages. We have therefore stored information incorrectly in terms of our needs, and we have caused a loss of information and potential consequences for our business users.

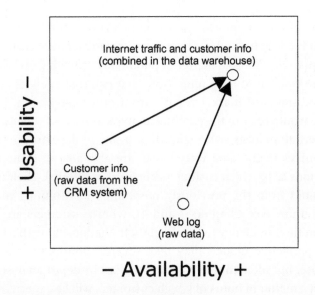

EXHIBIT 6.3 Synergy through the Combining of Data

Finally, the model also repeats the advantages of combining data correctly, because this enables us to obtain synergies. If we combine Web log information with master data, users' ages, gender, and any other information, we can carry out detailed studies for different groups of users and thus segmentations that mean we are getting even more value from our source data. This is also often referred to as one version of the truth; as opposed to the many versions of the truth that analysts create, when each in their own way combine data from a fragmented system landscape into reports. (See Exhibit 6.3.)

WHEN THERE IS MORE THAN ONE WAY TO GET THE JOB DONE

In large organizations we often see a two-tier business analytics function, namely the market analysts and the data warehouse analysts. The two groups are sometimes called, respectively, external analysts and internal analysts, based on their information sources. External analysts typically work with questionnaire analyses and interviews with direct contact with customers. This is what we call *primary data*, which is data collected for a given purpose. If we want to know which customers are disloyal, let's ask them. One of the problems with this kind of analysis is that it is costly to send out questionnaires to an entire customer base every quarter. It's also a matter of potentially annoying our customers with the constant questioning. Note that external analysts also often purchase standard market reports from other companies, in which case we would refer to the external analysts as users of *secondary data.*

Internal analysts, who take their point of departure in internal data sources in the data warehouse, are also able to come up with suggestions as to which customers are loyal or disloyal. Their information comes from the previously mentioned data mining models to predict churn (see Chapters 3 and 4), where customers are profiled based on their tendency to break off their relationship with a business. Churn predictive models may take several months to develop and automate, but after they are completed, an in-depth analysis can be made in a matter of hours of which customers will be expected to leave the business when and why. Moreover, they have the advantage of providing answers from all customers, so to speak, unlike questionnaire analyses, which are often completed by no more than 20% to 30% of customers in three weeks' time.

So, which solution do you choose? At the end of the day, the important thing is which solution is going to be more profitable in the long run. Do the internal analysts have the information about customers that can describe why these customers canceled their relationship with us? If not, the analysis is not going to add much value. In connection with some tasks we, the authors, performed for a major telecom company, we sent private customers a questionnaire about their loyalty, the results of which were used to carry out a churn predictive model. Based on the questionnaire analysis, we divided the respondents into four groups, depending on how loyal they scored themselves. Similarly, we could categorize our data, based on the percentage that describes the risk of losing a customer next month—which is one of the main results of a churn analysis. We divided the entire customer base into four segments, according to risk score from the churn analysis and let the groups be percentagewise as large as the ones that came out as a result of the questionnaire analysis. We then compared the efficiency of the two methods and were able to conclude that they were equally good at predicting which customers would leave next month. So the choice here was simple. Data mining provided a score for all customers within 24 hours without annoying any customers—and at considerably lower cost. In other situations, when we do not have as much information about customers as a telecom company does and a smaller customer base, questionnaire analyses may be the better option. What's important here is that it's not a question of *either/or*, or necessarily of *both/and*, but of what is more profitable in the given situation.

Likewise, it's important to look at the two information sources as supplementing each other, rather than as competing with each other in the organization. What really matters is not where we get our information, but how we apply it. As an example, say that we're working with the implementation of a CRM strategy with the overall objective of increasing our average revenue per customer. In this case, it doesn't matter whether it's a so-called basket analysis that constitutes the basis for decision or whether it's in-depth interviews or questionnaire analyses that form the foundation of the added-sales strategy we're implementing. What matters is that we make the right decisions in our cross-sales strategy.

In some cases, having overlapping information can even be an advantage. In connection with data mining models, which look to predict which customers the company will lose when and why, an exit analysis that, on a monthly basis, asks a number of customers who have canceled their commitment is able to systematically validate whether the statistical model is sufficient. If our interviewing tells us that a large number of customers are dissatisfied with the treatment they receive in our call center, then we know that our statistical model should include call center information and hints about how the data should be cut for the prediction modes. In this case, the external analysis function is thus able to support the analysis with a validation of the models.

WHEN THE QUALITY OF SOURCE DATA FAILS

In our discussion of data quality, we explained how organizations with high data quality use data as a valuable asset, which ensures competitiveness, boosts efficiency, improves customer service, and drives profitability. Alternatively, organizations with poor data quality spend much time working with contradictory reports—deviating business plans (budgets), which leads to misguided decisions based on dated, inconsistent, and erroneous figures. There is, in other words, a strong business case for improved data quality. The question in this section is how organizations can work efficiently to improve the data quality in their source systems (when data is created).

Poor data quality in source systems often becomes evident in connection with profiling, when data is combined in the data warehouse, and the trace leads from there to the source system. In order to efficiently improve data quality, we need to start at the source with validation. For instance, it should not be possible to enter information in the ERP system without selecting an account—it must be obligatory to fill in the account field. If this is not the case, mistakes will sometimes be made that compromise financial reporting. In terms of sales transactions, both customer number and customer name must be filled in. If these details are not registered, we can't know, for example, where to send the goods. Data quality can typically be improved significantly by making it obligatory to fill in important fields in the source systems. Business transactions should simply not go through, if all required fields are not completed.

Another well-known data quality problem arises when the same data is entered twice into one or more source systems. In many international organizations customers are set up and maintained in a local language and alphabet source system as well as in an English system. The first system can handle specific letters like the double letter *s* that is used in the German language or the special letters used in Scandinavia; the other can't. The solution is, of course, to design the system so as to ensure that customer data can be entered and maintained in one place only.

The keys to improved data quality in source systems are to improve the company's validation procedures when data is created, and to hold a firm principle to create and maintain data in one place only.

SUMMARY

In this chapter we went through typical data-generating systems in the business's immediate environment and the difference between primary and secondary data, as well as external and internal analyses. We looked at initiatives to improve the data quality of source systems. Finally, we present a way in which a business can prioritize which source systems to collect project-related data from.

We also explained that if you do not see the potential in source data, you will not be able to lead your business with confidence into the future using information as a strategic resource.

CHAPTER **7**

Structuring of a Business Intelligence Competency Center

I n Chapter 6, we looked at the business's creation of source data and thus completed our presentation of the business analytics (BA) model from Chapter 1. In this chapter, we discuss how the activities of the BA model can be carried out via a business intelligence competency center (BICC).

WHAT IS A BUSINESS INTELLIGENCE COMPETENCY CENTER?

A BICC is a forum that includes analytical and business competencies as well as IT competencies. This combination of competencies ensures that BA has the necessary impact on the organization. The establishment of a BICC is based on experiences that show barriers in relation to competencies and organizational structure to be the most limiting factor when it comes to the successful creation and execution of BA.

The creation of a BICC is the establishment of an organizational entity, which includes different competencies across the organization and which becomes a problem-solving forum. Its purpose is to maximize the revenue flow from business analytics initiatives and to make BA a business process, rather than an IT process. In other words, a BICC works to ensure that the business's needs drive all technical initiatives, thereby making sure that the business does not get a data warehouse with a life of its own, independent of the needs of the business. Similarly, a BICC works to ensure that the business realizes the potential benefits of BA, and to ensure that the necessary analytical competencies are present and accessible. That, by the way, is entirely in line with our BA model from Chapter 1.

WHY SET UP A BUSINESS INTELLIGENCE COMPETENCY CENTER?

Typically, companies that create a BICC want the BA function to have more impact. Often there are quite a few analysts in large organizations, but they are spread out in different departments and divisions and they have no common forum. This means that problems that the individual analyst has extraordinary scope for solving will only be formulated locally in his or her department, depending on the analyst's ability to promote the ideas and depending on whether these ideas are compatible with local strategies and management preferences.

If, however, we gather analysts and the closest related competencies—which we will look at in the following section—into one single organizational entity, this entity might now have a voice so strong it can be heard throughout the organization. This can be done in either of two ways. The first is by giving the manager of the BICC a formal influence on and access to management forums, where both the potential as well as any problems in connection with BA can be addressed in a strategic context. The second way a BICC will be able to create synergies is at the functional level. An analyst with data mining competencies placed in marketing will be able to see and promote the potential of data mining methodology in human resources via dialogue with the analyst from human resources. In other words, the purpose of a BICC is to give the BA function the critical mass to be heard at a strategic level as well as to create synergies at an operational level.

One element that we also will address in this chapter for the first time is knowledge management, so that we now will deal with three Ls: lead, lag, and learning information.

The overall argument for the establishment of a BICC is that it is a precondition for an efficient linking of the business's strategy with a BA strategy. If analysts are spread around different departments without a common forum, the IT/data warehouse section, on the one hand, and the business, on the other hand, have very poor chances of establishing an ongoing dialogue. It's an essential part of the analyst's function to build a bridge between specified business needs and the data warehouse via an understanding of which methodology and which data once combined can fulfill the needs. If the company does not have an analytical function to link the business and IT, the result of the dialogue will, in all likelihood, become a large number of technical solutions, which are created without insight into the best method of generating knowledge and information. Since the rest of the organization will still require decision support, they will then start building work-arounds in order to get access to the data they need. Worst case they will stop using the data warehouse completely or only as a provider of lag information.

TASKS AND COMPETENCIES

In this section, we take a closer look at which tasks and therefore also which competencies are required in a BICC. As always, we want to emphasize that competence profiles are not individuals, but roles. One person may well fulfill several roles. For example, a data miner will typically be statistically knowledgeable, and thereby able to take on two roles or competence areas. Likewise, an IT-oriented person may well have business and strategic insight, too. Similarly, a competence profile could easily require a combination of several employees.

Establishing an Information Wheel

The primary task for a BICC is to deliver the right information and the right knowledge to the right people at the right time. This is the whole

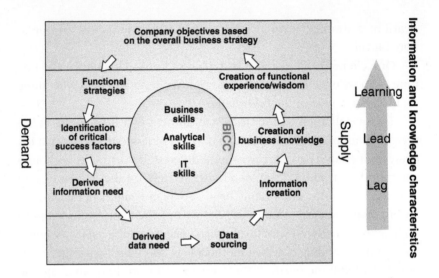

EXHIBIT 7.1 The Information Wheel: From Demand to Supply of Business Support

definition of BA used in this book. In other words, it's a question of keeping the information wheel turning, as shown in Exhibit 7.1. The information wheel sums up the concepts that were described in Chapters 2 through 6: First we specify which knowledge and which information the business requires based on its chosen strategy. Data is then retrieved and condensed to information and knowledge, which is delivered to users. In the model we have introduced the concept of *wisdom*, which refers to *knowledge management*, which seeks to create and retain learning over time—in this context to be activated at a strategic level.

Knowledge management is essentially being able to summarize overall learning about how you establish, improve, maintain, or close down business processes and store them for the use of others. One common feature across strategies is that they have the tendency of centralizing company activities to capture and benefit from local skills and make use of these organization-wide. It is also not uncommon that a few years later, another decentralization strategy is presented with the purpose of releasing the creativity of the organization. Over time this can be seen as a strategic heartbeat that keeps organizations adapting to new market conditions via decentralizing and implementing them organization-wide during the next centralization strategy. It is, however, a very costly maneuver for an international organization to make strategy changes at this level, and this is where knowledge management comes in. The purpose of knowledge management is to have the best of both: a decentralized organization releasing its full creative potential while at the same time making sure that other decentralized units reuse the good ideas generated.

In the simplest form, this could be done via a follow-up procedure on all campaigns: A document is created that describes the campaigns, how they were managed, and what their results were (lead and lag information). Now a business unit in France can make a search on how to make a cross-selling campaign toward small customers and be given decision support on how they did in, say, Ghana, Brazil, and China. Not only might France get knowledge "person-to-paper," but they might be able to see who actually executed the campaigns and contact these "person-to-person." Suddenly we have created task-specific virtual networks that, say, a strategy team could rely on, as shown in the information wheel in Exhibit 7.1. In smaller organizations this could mean making public knowledge that is specific to a person and making that knowledge sustainable across generations of employees and jobholders.

As discussed here, we are talking about many information wheels that need to be established and maintained, typically one per business process that is based on BA information.

Creating Synergies between Information Wheels

The BICC must therefore establish and maintain these information wheels, but at the same time we should be clear that the processes illustrated in the information wheel are not necessarily performed in just one place in the organization; they can easily be performed in several places. The person responsible for CRM activities wants to generate customer information to monitor activities. So does the person responsible for sales in connection with the planning and monitoring of sales activities. The same thing is true in connection with human resources, production, logistics, procurement, and others. In this context, people talk about the occurrence of information islands or the silo syndrome, which occurs when the different business units create and maintain their BA systems without any coordination.

Not surprisingly, this results in different terminologies, technology strategies, and procedures across the organization. This leads to the creation of data redundancy and knowledge-sharing barriers, resulting in a considerable amount of uncoordinated tactical BA projects, each delivering limited insight and effect on the bottom line.

One of the most important tasks of a BICC is therefore to coordinate all these information wheels in order to create synergy on the data side via a correct combining of data. In addition, synergies must be created across analysts (knowledge sharing among analysts) as well as synergies on the IT side. As an example, it has been estimated that software costs could be reduced by approximately 25% if solutions were standardized via fewer platforms, which would also give the organization a better negotiating position as a major customer with software vendors. A similar number is mentioned in relation to costs in terms of external consultants and employees, since a reduced number of technologies means that the organization does not need to have expertise in as many technologies and can therefore minimize the number of integration projects. The number can, of course, be formulated positively; we get proportionally more performance for the money we pay consultants and staff in our IT department.

As illustrated in Exhibit 7.2, a BICC must assume responsibility for the establishment of an ongoing dialogue between the business and IT to ensure that the chosen information architecture and the chosen technologies support the information strategy. *Information architecture* describes the ways in which we move data and information around the organization, while the *technologies* refers to the software and hardware solutions that will subsequently perform the task. This terminol-

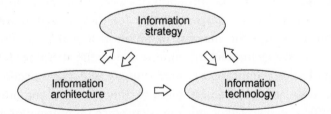

EXHIBIT 7.2 Interrelationships between Information Strategy, Information Architecture, and Information Technology

ogy corresponds perfectly with the definition of BA used in this book; otherwise the right people won't be getting the right information at the right time, as part of an automated process. As illustrated in Exhibit 7.2, we first set up our information architecture. Only then can we formulate the requirements to individual technological solutions—both individually and combined. We would like to stress that a BICC does not design information architecture or technology strategies. This is the system owners' job. A BICC enters into a dialogue with the system owners to ensure that the chosen information architecture and the chosen systems support the organization's information strategy. If this does not happen, we find ourselves again in the situation where the scope of the BA function is determined by technological solutions rather than by the information needs of the business.

Educating Users

It's perfectly possible to have a good technological solution supporting the information strategy, and yet not be adding value. That's just a question of not using it. If there are no users, there will not be any improved decision making, and thereby no value creation as a result of the solution. In BA, a solution is never better than its users. If we want successful implementation of BA solutions, a rule of thumb is that three elements need to be in place: user-friendliness, relevant information, and general support.

In terms of *user-friendliness*, the system must be inviting, intuitive, and clear. This is best achieved by asking the users themselves for input in relation to design. A simple solution like a report requires only one or two feedback processes between the BICC and the end users. A more complicated system that must support many business processes and many users in a changing business environment requires much more in terms of user interface and flexibility. We must therefore expect that the system will be developed in an ongoing dialogue with the business. In other words, we wouldn't start the programming of the different modules, until their design was discussed with and approved by the users.

The *relevance of the information* is what comes out of the system. The format doesn't matter if the contents of the system are of no value. Here we can refer to another rule of thumb, which is that information—with the point of departure being the users' perspective—must be available, accurate, and actionable. If it takes a long time for the user to obtain the required information, the information cannot be said to be accessible and users are therefore wasting their time. Similarly, the information must be precise in order that users dare to base their decisions on it. Solutions obviously need to deliver useful information in relation to the business process they're supporting.

When implementing new information systems, *general support* means that users should be trained in using them, if we want them to actually do so. Equally, users must have easy access to support, which means that if they have questions or suggestions for improvements, they will be listened to.

If user-friendliness, relevance of information, and general support do not live up to the users' needs and expectations, user satisfaction will drop and so will the use of the systems. This constitutes a nonstarter situation, simply because the solution was not based on the users' needs. We have created a BA system to assist with a business need, but it doesn't work, because the solution we've created has failed in one or more of the previous three dimensions.

All this brings us back to the fact that the delivery of BA information is a chain that is only as strong as its weakest link. And if the system is used only half as much as expected, it has lost half its value. The costs, however, remain the same—plus a further weariness in relation to BA solutions.

Prioritizing New BA Initiatives

The final major role of a BICC is to coordinate and prioritize new BA initiatives. Since we consider this to be a key issue, we have reserved a separate chapter (Chapter 8) for this subject.

Competencies

A BICC must contain all the tasks already described. Typically, these are divided into three domains. Exhibit 7.3 shows the three domains as well as which tasks might lie in each of these and their intersections.

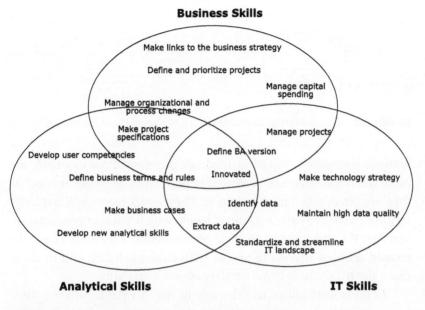

EXHIBIT 7.3 Competency Areas and Types of Tasks in a BICC

We've included this exhibit because there is a difference between the competencies that are needed in a BICC and the way in which information moves about in an organization, which is described via the information wheel. The information wheel is based on considerable preparatory work, created, among other things, via the performance of the tasks described in Exhibit 7.3.

CENTRALIZED OR DECENTRALIZED ORGANIZATION

The establishment of a BICC can be carried out by creating a new formal organizational entity. It can be created, too, by establishing it as a virtual organization. This is illustrated in Exhibit 7.4. On the left-hand side of the exhibit, a BICC is shown as an organizational support function, which indicates that the BICC is given a strategic role in its work. On the right-hand side of the exhibit, a BICC is established as a virtual function. This indicates that the department to a lesser extent is given a strategic role and to a greater extent has been created as an analytical forum to facilitate synergies, and that focus is on strengthening the BA function at an operational level. This interpretation, however, is not

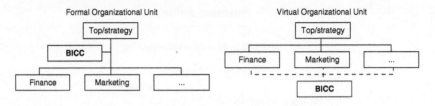

EXHIBIT 7.4 BICC as a Formal Organizational Unit or a Virtual Organizational Unit

without exceptions. Small or medium businesses, for example, are more likely to make use of virtual departments or "work teams," as they are often called in this context. These work teams will naturally contain members with a strategic focus, which ensures coordination between BA and strategy. In large organizations, a BICC can easily be created without involving people with strategic focus, and in these cases, the BICC can become a purely operational entity.

As previously illustrated, the way in which we establish our BICC is not of vital importance. It's a question of the organization's ambitions for it. As always we have to ask ourselves the key question: What are we trying to achieve with this change? In this case, the answer will be along the lines of either more strategic focus or simply just an increased performance.

Strategy or Performance

As always, when a new business initiative is launched, we must assess whether it supports the company's strategy or the company's performance or both. If it does neither, we should wonder whether we have lost track of what we are trying to accomplish. Similarly, in connection with the activities of the BA function, we must ask ourselves whether the aim is to optimize the company's performance, or whether the aim is to achieve a closer relationship between the company's strategy and the way in which information is used.

If we focus first on how to improve our performance, the aim is to be more proactive at an operational level, as illustrated by Exhibit 7.5. A good example of a reactive operational BA function would be if our procedures are based on users coming to us. They order the information or knowledge they need, and then we agree on a deadline of, say,

Strategic focus

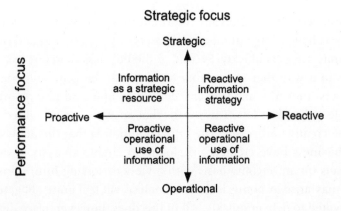

EXHIBIT 7.5 Performance and Strategy

three days for delivery. On the face of it, all seems fine here. But try looking at it from the business's point of view. Let's say they are in a creative meeting, and at one point they are having discussions where they want to know how many of their customers in a given region have a consumption of over $400 per month. They can have their answer, of course; it just takes three days. The next time marketing is in a creative situation, they are not going to use the BA function to answer questions like that; they simply do not have the time to wait, unless it's an absolutely vital question. The result is that the business uses the BA function less because of the long response time. Maybe the business chooses to use the BA function in only 30% of all the cases it was expected to be used, when the BA function was established. All of a sudden, we have a situation where the BA function either represents a bottleneck or where the business completely avoids using it. Business support and thereby improved decision making is reduced to 30% and, with that, the value creation based on the data warehouse. We are not getting return on investment from our data warehouse.

One way of improving the BA department's performance is to make sure that its analysts participate in meetings that will result in the business subsequently drawing on them as a resource. First, this means that analysts can advise on which data in combination with which methods will deliver optimum results in relation to any given problems. This constitutes an ongoing briefing of the analysts, which in turn means that they will be working in a more targeted way with the delivery of the relevant information and knowledge. Typically, analysts have a large number of datasets or programs at hand that can generate answers quickly. Second, if the business therefore asks questions in a way that means that answers can be generated via these datasets, then the analysts can deliver complex ad hoc reports in a couple of hours or less. This means that answers can be a direct result of the creative processes. The only condition is that the analysts and the business have created a dialogue to enable analysts to develop datasets on an ongoing basis with a view to solving future problems that may arise. A bonus is that an analyst will feel more obligated and motivated to deliver quickly. All of this does, however, place demands on the analyst's business insight or tool kit, as explained in Chapter 4.

The previous scenario means that analysts must be included in the work teams that draw on their resources. If the company wishes to go down this route, a virtual BICC is sufficient. The analyst will be ensured direct access to the end-users of the decision support that they generate and can become involved in the development of the value-creating processes. Equally, analysts are given a common forum, which means that they can complement each other's competencies.

If the objective of a BICC is to achieve a closer integration between the BA function and the company's strategy, we've got a strong case for the establishment of the BICC as a formal organizational entity. The primary argument is the impact it gives to have a BICC manager, who can focus on this project and who has a number of employees working for him or her as direct resources that can come into play. If the person responsible for the BICC does not have the formal authority to prioritize strategic tasks, a lot of the analysts' time will be spent on the operational tasks they're performing for their respective departments. At the same time, IT competencies' time in a BICC will be spent on data warehouse maintenance rather than working on enabling what the commercial side of the organization requires.

Further steps toward the goal are to identify where the organization is currently, and where it would like to be. In Chapter 2, we designed a model showing different degrees of integration between the organization's strategy and the deployment of BA. The model can be used as inspiration for this analysis. Alternatively, a "maturity analysis" can be ordered from most IT consultancy firms, and this can lift the dialogue further. Maturity analyses are usually built on a description of current information systems based on a number of dimensions, such as technical elements, people competencies, and the business processes they must support. Similarly, a description is made of the information systems which, in relation to strategies, must be built on the same dimensions. Where we are and where we want to be are thus found— and the problem has been broken down into a number of dimensions, which makes everything clearer.

When organizational clarity has been established about where we are and where we want to be, the next analysis looks at whether we've got the necessary resources and competencies to move from (a) to (b). As mentioned previously, information systems can be divided into three dimensions:

1. Technical elements, where the question is: Are we internally in possession of the technical leverage which may be required?

2. People elements, where the question is: Are we internally in possession of the competencies and resources to solve the analytical tasks and train users in future solutions as required?

3. Business process elements, where the question is: Are we organized businesswise in such a way that we will get full value from our new strategic BA initiatives? Just as the term *maturity assessment* is used to describe where we are and where we should be going, the term *readiness assessment* is used in connection with an analysis of whether we as an organization are ready to move from where we are to where we want to be. After these two analyses, we've answered the two questions: Where should we be going? And how do we get there?

When the Analysts Reports to the IT Department

The alternative to analysts being employed in the business is to place them under the IT function. This structure has its obvious weaknesses, since we're turning the whole value chain upside down, so that analysts go from requesting information and knowledge based on business problems to offering information based on what's accessible in the data warehouse—in direct opposition to our BA model. The difference occurs, amongst other things, because analysts' time now becomes prioritized by the data warehouse section's management. This means that analyst competencies move from solving business problems to taking their point of departure in the data warehouse universe. It's a question of employee loyalty, too. When the analyst acts in a gray area between the business and IT, where should the analyst place his or her loyalty? Should it be with the business that insists IT must find a different way of doing things or with IT that insists that's not possible?

The answer should be considered in relation to the overall purpose of establishing a data warehouse in the first place (i.e., to improve the business's decision making). It is therefore an integrated part of the analyst's role to constantly challenge the data warehouse on behalf of the business in terms of the quality of the solutions he or she delivers. This is not different from what goes on elsewhere in companies. If the sales department is dissatisfied with the products that are produced or the advertisements that are developed, they must be able to object. Equally, people who deliver and implement sold solutions must be able to raise concerns with sales, if they promise more than the organization can deliver. Also, finance must be able to interfere if sales is pricing products too cheaply, so even though they may be selling enough, the business is not making money. There are, in other words, a large number of value chains in an organization, all of which result in the delivery of services to customers. If these value chains are turned upside down, or rather, if we create an organization where there is no correlation between responsibility and value chains, we take away the platform for quality assurance.

If the sales manager is responsible for the delivery and implementation of sold solutions, with whom do technicians then take the critical dialogue, if the sales manager won't acknowledge that customers are actually being promised more than the organization can deliver? Technicians then have the option of approaching the next management level. This involves a real risk of being fired and, anyway, it won't be a great career move for the individual employee who's actually risking his own neck for the good of the organization. We therefore find ourselves in a situation where we have an unhelpful correlation between the value chain and the responsibility for the quality of this value chain. And if the problem is not solved, our customers will suffer as a result of the lack of internal quality in sales and delivery processes.

The same thing happens in an organization if the value chain is arranged in such a way that analysts owe their loyalty to the data warehouse and not to the business. The only difference is that nobody complains. In the data warehouse framework (which is the business), customers will find it very difficult to formulate arguments for what can be done without the analysts' competencies. As a result, the analysts will have no option but to keep quiet.

The reason why consideration should be given to establishing a BICC as an independent business entity is that it's a way of giving BA the necessary organizational impact at a strategic level and the potential synergies this will render at an operational level. Consideration should be given, too, to how this business entity is embedded, to ensure the correlation between the organization's value chains and the responsibility for the quality of these value chains. This reasoning applies long term as well, so that a change of management will not put the BICC at risk of coming under technically oriented management. As we stated at the beginning of this chapter, consideration should be given to whether the company's strategy and performance are supported by placing a BICC in the technically oriented part of the organization.

WHEN SHOULD A BICC BE ESTABLISHED?

As discussed previously in this chapter, we'll split up this question: Is the primary purpose of establishing a BICC to optimize day-to-day business processes at an operational level, or is it to achieve a closer integration between the company's strategy and the way in which information is used? If the establishment of a BICC has the primary purpose of achieving improvements at an operational level (performance), then the BICC can be established as a virtual organization, as already discussed. The BICC should also work to ensure that analysts are placed as centrally as possible in connection with the decision process at a departmental level. An obvious time to establish a virtual organization would be in connection with the start-up of new data warehouse projects, since analysts would be able to contribute with requirement specifications in terms of which information to collect in the future and in which format.

Even more relevant is whether it would be in connection with the completion of a data warehouse project, where new information is made available to the organization. If, so the creation of a new virtual organization could work as a kick-off for the new data warehouse project. But there are other reasons why the creation of a BICC would be a good idea at this time, especially if external consultants have been in on the project. At the end of the project, these consultants will typically leave the organization, taking with them considerable knowledge about subjects such as these: Why did we structure the data warehouse as we did? Which departments and functions in the business requested which information and in which format? To whom should the BA function then start its deliveries? Do we as the BA department have the necessary analytical competencies to meet the organization's information requirements? Do we even have the necessary analytical software? Then there's the issue of being able to navigate the new data warehouse. We must therefore ensure a transfer of SQL code to enable our analyst to use all the tables in the new data warehouse from day one. A data warehouse is an information system like any other. If analysts cannot use its full potential, we're already taking a value loss.

Another argument for establishing a BICC in connection with the kick-off of new data warehouse projects is amusingly explained by Douglas Adams. In his book, *The Hitchhiker's Guide to the Galaxy* (Del Rey, 2010), a civilization on a planet would like an answer to "the ultimate question of life, the universe, and everything." To that aid, they build a computer that provides the answer millions of years later. The problem is that the civilization forgets the question in the meantime and therefore has to make a new computer, which for additional millions of years will be calculating which question had been put forward, after the original computer had delivered the answer. There are strong parallels here to what may happen in an organization: Some years ago, when the data warehouse project was launched, the business was interviewed about which information they might want in relation to its different business processes. The problem with this is that not a soul is able to remember this now. The analysts are therefore asked to investigate the potential of the new data warehouse for the business. This is where a knowledge transfer should have happened, when the project was completed—from the people who made the initial requirement specification to the data warehouse to its users: the business and the analysts.

We also mentioned the concept of knowledge management. In essence this will force the BICC to focus on what the business demands and will potentially give the BICC the task of promoting a knowledge library including a methodological way of gathering learning from the organization. At the same time, the BICC must be an active creator and provider of decision support to the strategic level.

Another good time for a company to establish a BICC is when people at a strategic level realize that information can be used as a strategic resource in the given competitive environment. Who will now drive the process further? It's important to note here that these situations often require much more than analytical resources. It takes insight into strategy and the strategy development process to adapt the right BA initiatives to a strategic context. Moreover, we've got a *change management* task to perform. That is, we often need to address the soft issues, such as the corporate culture. We now need to train the entire organization in when it's supposed to deploy factual decision making based on BA information—and equally, when it's not expected to do so. New attitudes must be taught, formed, and strengthened. And similarly, we need to challenge, transform, and dissolve old and reluctant attitudes via positive learning processes. Further, the organization must understand the importance of data quality. If the people in sales do not enter their prospects in the CRM system, then the CRM system itself is a wasted investment. If customer names are not entered carefully, we won't be able to find them later. We have to find and reward good examples of fact-based decisions, promote these in the rest of the organization, and also point out incorrect or insufficient use of the established information systems. It's important, too, to continually ensure that management at all levels is supporting the implementation of this kind of decision making, since their role as advocates is significant to the successful implementation of the project.

If this does not happen, we risk getting into a vicious circle, where the system has no users, or where data is used unsystematically, which again will result in poor data quality. Poor data quality will be evident, when information may be accessible, but it is imprecise and irrelevant. This will make users even more reluctant to use the information systems and the entire information strategy; they now look like a failed project, which will lose its sponsors at an overall management level. We cannot stress enough the fact that an organization is made up of people. And since they are the ones who must change their behavior, it's a critical success factor for the project to be able to win, retain, and develop their commitment to the project. The technical part is the easier part of the project. The soft part (the people part) is the tough one.

SUMMARY

In this chapter, looked at how the activities of the BA model can be carried out via a business intelligence competency center.

A BICC is a forum that includes analytical and business competencies as well as IT competencies and works to ensure that it's the needs of the business that drive all technical initiatives, thereby making sure that the business does not get a data warehouse with a life of its own. One of the most important tasks of a BICC is to coordinate information wheels in order to create synergy on the data side, as well as synergies across analysts and IT professionals.

If the objective of a BICC is to achieve a closer integration between the BA function and the company's strategy, we recommended the establishment of the BICC as a formal organizational entity. However, if the objective of a BICC is to optimize the company's performance, we recommended the establishment of the BICC as a virtual organizational unit.

CHAPTER 8

Assessment and Prioritization of BA Projects

The question of how to prioritize business analytics (BA) projects leads to two more questions: In which order should the BA initiatives be implemented? and Which initiatives should not be implemented at all? In the radio station case study in Chapter 1, we used one simple financial rule of thumb as our business case. That rule decided that the project *should* be implemented. Assessing BA initiatives in the real world, however, is somewhat more complicated. To answer the above two questions, we'll use a business case. A *business case* is an analytical tool that can provide support to decisions about whether to implement a BA project.

IS IT A STRATEGIC PROJECT OR NOT?

When prioritizing projects, it's important to decide whether a given project is strategic. If it is, we don't have to assess whether the project should be carried out on the basis of a business case. Rather, we must expect this assessment to have been undertaken already from the strategic side. We do, however, have to ensure that sufficient means have been set aside for the project and, if this is not the case, we must decide which budgets are to cover the costs of the project.

However, if the project is not specified as part of the company's strategy, it means that it is requested based on the expectation that it will render improved business performance. This is called a *bottom up–driven initiative* because it comes from the operational environment. The opposite is called a *top down–driven initiative*, which is activated from the strategy.

Typically, projects that are not initiated from the strategy are prioritized in relation to other projects based on a business case approach. A business case performs the simple math of relating costs to the financial gains of a project and, in this way, we can assess from a purely financial point of view whether we get the best return on investment. In Exhibit 8.1, we've made a small model showing how projects may be compared. This model is naturally not exhaustive, but can assist in creating an overview of different project candidates and their different natures.

If we have a project with low costs and a high return, this project will obviously be preferred to a project with the same costs, but less return. Likewise, projects with high costs and low return would be rejected. A final possibility is a project with high value creation and high resource consumption. In this case, an assessment should be made of whether the project can be lifted up into a strategic context and, if not, whether it is then still relevant. It goes without saying that a project like that will take up a lot of resources in the departments that will be responsible for its implementation. In other words, even if there is a positive business case for the project, it may be necessary to dismiss it due to its demand on resources and the fact that the project

		Costs	
		Low	**High**
Benefits	**High**	Gold mine	Align with strategy
	Low	Maybe	Not interesting

EXHIBIT 8.1 Business Analytics Project Costs Compared with Benefits

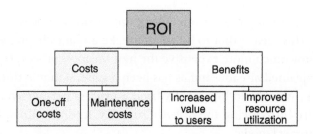

EXHIBIT 8.2 Return on Investment (ROI)

process will affect the company's agility adversely. By *agility* we mean the ability to make fast decisions, and to respond quickly to new opportunities, which could be golden opportunities, resulting from the implementation period of this major project. The large project therefore entails certain opportunity costs for the organization during its implementation. That is, we must weigh the added value of any golden opportunities that must be disregarded, as well as the opportunity to quickly start up strategic initiatives that may turn up along the way.

As illustrated in Exhibit 8.1, we can build a business case on the weighting of financial advantages and disadvantages of the business case. In Exhibit 8.2, we break this down even further, as an introduction to the following sections, which are about costs and advantages, respectively.

First, Exhibit 8.2 points out that costs related to the implementation of IT solutions are rarely one-off costs; we're typically looking at some additional future costs. Second, the exhibit shows that we must separate and arrange these according to increased value for the users of the system and in savings, when we look at the advantages created by a given project.

UNCOVERING THE VALUE CREATION OF THE PROJECT

The difficult thing about making business cases for BA projects is that they do not create value in themselves. Only when the subsequent improved decision making is experienced, is value creation realized at an organizational level. It may therefore be tempting to list IT and implementation costs on the one hand and then a number of advantages on the other. But the truth is often more complicated than that, because we usually move from having one business process to having another. This means that to be able to make a real estimate, we must look at how much more expensive the new business process is going to be. As explained already, and as has been a general theme throughout this book, we should look at BA from a process perspective. That is why we're introducing the SIPOC (Supplier, Input, Process, Output, and Customer) model.

The model is used to describe a process. What we will do now is to describe a process before and after we've established a BA system, and then sum up: What are the one-off costs, what are differences in the cost of driving the process, and what is the added value on the output side—both for the process users and as a saving for the people executing the process?

In the following example, we have decided to carry out a BA initiative in a company that has many employees and that is finding it difficult to retain them. Historically, the company has had a process built on BA, based on recommendations from human resources (Supplier), having transformed data into some reports in the BA department via a reporting module (Input). This has resulted in a report (Output), which has been delivered to HR and top management (the customer or user of the process). (See Exhibit 8.3.) Reactions to these reports have been sporadic. They have been read, of course, but they have not prompted any direct or systematic actions. It's been more of a case of using the reports as an argument, if they were useful for individual stakeholders in a given situation. The process is described in the middle column, which is typically the first thing done. Based on this, we identify input and output in relation to the process, as well as who the suppliers and recipients are. Another advantage of describing the process in this way is that we clearly define what we are working with and identify all project stakeholders and their roles, influence, and interests.

The idea with this new business initiative is that we, through data mining, must identify which employees leave the company when and why. With that background, we can initiate retention initiatives, which could be individualized salary packages, education and training, dialogue with management, or considerations concerning the hiring of different employee profiles in the future. Also,

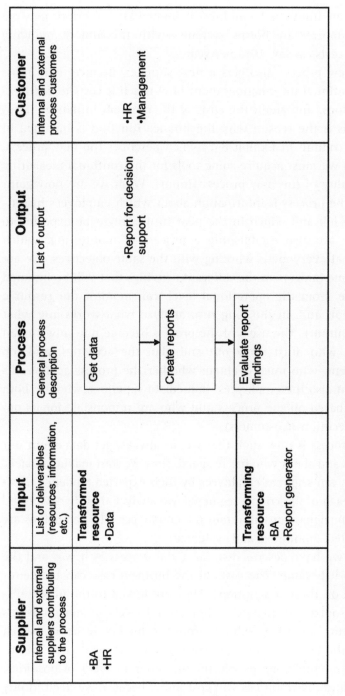

Supplier	Input	Process	Output	Customer
Internal and external suppliers contributing to the process	List of deliverables (resources, information, etc.)	General process description	List of output	Internal and external process customers
•BA •HR	**Transformed resource** •Data **Transforming resource** •BA •Report generator	Get data → Create reports → Evaluate report findings	•Report for decision support	•HR •Management

EXHIBIT 8.3   SIPOC Diagram Showing the Current Status of the Process

demands on individual employees' immediate superiors may be made—supported by bonus systems—with the aim of reducing employee costs by, say, 10% per year.

The new process also gets a new supplier, finance, who must deliver continual information about how much it costs to refill vacant positions, and about the costs of the different initiatives (Supplier). This is the reason why the finance function is included in the input column in Exhibit 8.4, which describes the new process. Moreover, we must acquire some tools for the continual measuring of the quality of the new process (Input). What we are now gaining from the process is information about which employees historically have left and which in the near future might be expected to leave. We are also establishing a process of monitoring, which ensures that everyone is working with the same objectives. We are linking some budgets to the different activities that will be initiated so that we, from the operational level, can monitor our resource consumption and, in the long run, analyze what works and what doesn't (Output). The users of the process become not only human resources, who must carry out and plan the activities, and top management, who must evaluate whether the process achieves its targets, but also the employees' immediate superiors, who are both rewarded based on the process and who are responsible for its operative execution (Customers).

The process is now such that we, as always, get data about our employees and about who has resigned. Now we start making models, too, which can segment employees by their expected tendency to resign. For each of the critical segments, we analyze their behavior and design campaigns that will retain the employees. The campaigns are implemented, monitored, and evaluated.

What we have described so far is the process as it was and the process as it became. The costs of the business case can be identified based on these descriptions. They are linked to the new transformed resources. In this case, they are relatively limited, since it's about getting some key exhibits from the finance function, which describes the budgets and some costing keys for what costs are involved in re-employing people for the different types of positions. The transforming resources will cost more, because we need to buy

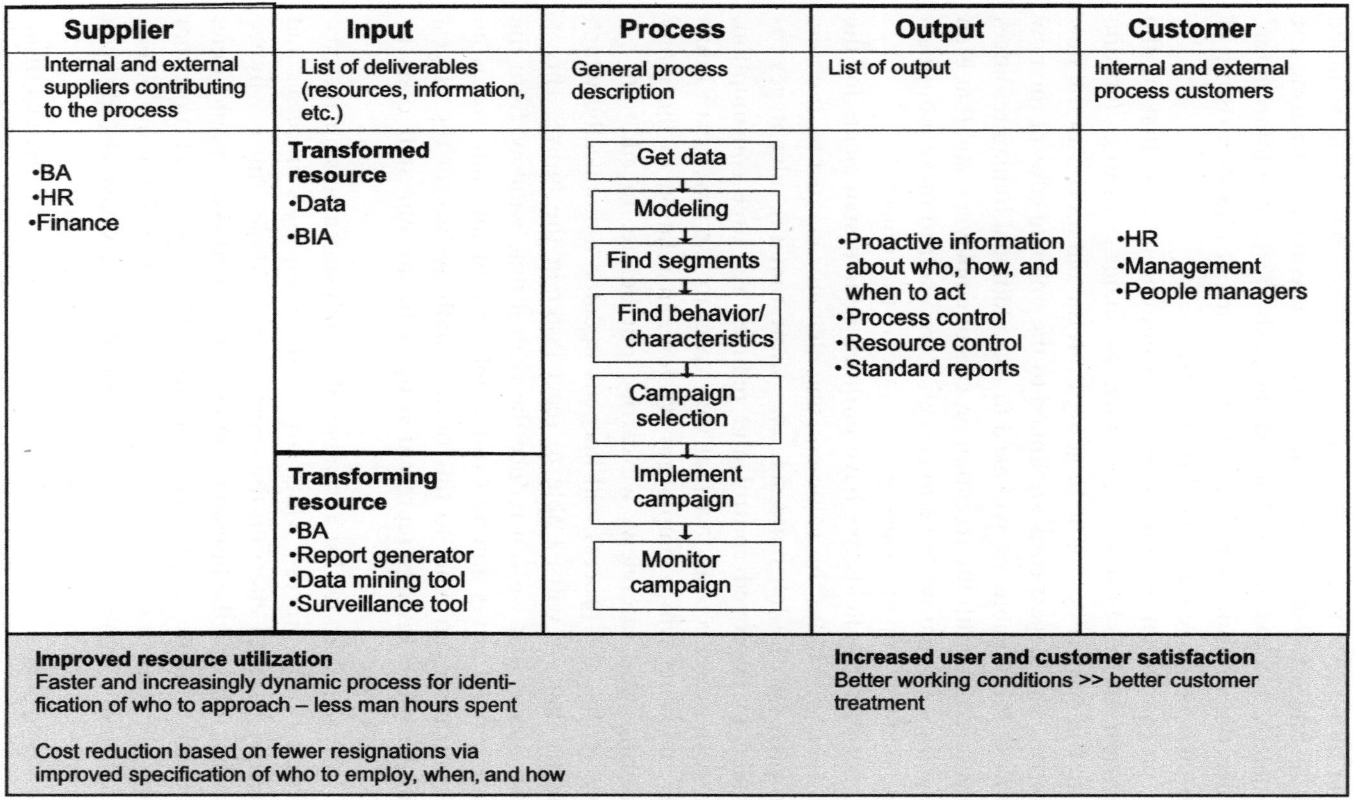

Supplier	Input	Process	Output	Customer
Internal and external suppliers contributing to the process	List of deliverables (resources, information, etc.)	General process description	List of output	Internal and external process customers
•BA •HR •Finance	**Transformed resource** •Data •BIA **Transforming resource** •BA •Report generator •Data mining tool •Surveillance tool	Get data → Modeling → Find segments → Find behavior/characteristics → Campaign selection → Implement campaign → Monitor campaign	•Proactive information about who, how, and when to act •Process control •Resource control •Standard reports	•HR •Management •People managers

Improved resource utilization
Faster and increasingly dynamic process for identification of who to approach – less man hours spent

Cost reduction based on fewer resignations via improved specification of who to employ, when, and how

Increased user and customer satisfaction
Better working conditions >> better customer treatment

EXHIBIT 8.4 SIPOC Diagram Showing the Process We Want to Create

data mining software and train internal users, which are assumed to be one-off costs. Moreover, costs are involved in training the people who are to use and act on the basis of the new information. Since the solution is within the framework of already existing IT systems, we have no costs of that type.

In conclusion, we can say that it is not one-off costs that are the heaviest for this business case, since the major costs in connection with this project do not lie in going from the old process to the new process. The biggest costs are linked to the ongoing costs of the new process. Presumably, we will need to use additional human resources in connection with the retention process of employees, and that is an ongoing cost that we have to accept, if we want to make a business case that sums up the ongoing advantages of the project.

In the gray fields, we have outlined benefit statements for the process, which are the value-creating elements created by the new process. On the left-hand side, we show that the advantages included in improved control and reduced resource consumption. First, these reflect the fact that we expect to use fewer man hours for analyzing which employees we lose, in relation to the many meetings and interviews we carried out before. In addition, we expect that the process will keep us updated dynamically, which means that we will be able to react faster in the future. This in turn means that we can reduce the critical time window, from the time a need arises amongst our employees to the time we as an organization can react to this need. Finally we've got the biggest number—the savings represented by reducing our staff costs by 10% per year.

On the right, we list a number of benefit statements for the customers of the process, which are all the company's processes and thereby have an effect on the company as a whole. This is why we haven't included the human resources department as a customer here. You might argue that human resources will be better off, now that they are receiving more precise information from BA about which employees resigned and why. But these advantages have already been included in the cost reductions in terms of reducing staff costs by 10%. However, there are also other results that can be derived from improved working conditions for employees. For one thing, they give better customer relations. This is therefore included as another result of our process improvement.

Based on the identified advantages, we can calculate their value in exact exhibits. Naturally, the person responsible for the business case cannot always put a value on relatively abstract quantities such as the customer loyalty effect. In that case we will have to ask the customer relationship management (CRM) department.

Exhibit 8.5 sums up where to find the different elements for a business case via a SIPOC model. The white fields contain cost elements, which in this context focus on dividing costs in one-off costs and ongoing costs, respectively. The gray fields are still showing the advantages delivered by the new process to the company, which for one thing entails that we use the information in a new way. The black fields are not included, but might have contained information about who achieved savings and who gained added value from the process. Finally, the output field will tell us what the new output was specifically, but not its value. That is why it is blacked out.

WHEN PROJECTS RUN OVER SEVERAL YEARS

Generally speaking, business cases for BA projects should be presented with a calculation of the present value of the project. This is due to the fact that the establishment of BA projects along with their subsequent effects may have a span of many years. If, for instance, we establish a project that must finance itself over the next ten years, we have a financial outlay, which we must take into consideration. We may go out and borrow the money, which means we pay interest to a bank until the project has paid for itself. Alternatively, we may have the money ourselves already, but we tie it up in the project and incur opportunity cost equal to what this money could have earned us had it been invested in another project. Therefore the net present value (NPV) is often calculated for BA projects.

NPV is calculated by discounting all financial costs with an interest rate that cancels out capital costs and is adjusted according to the risk of the project. And only if the calculated NPV of the project is positive should we consider implementing the project.

Supplier	Input	Process	Output	Customer
Internal and external suppliers contributing to the process	List of deliverables (resources, information, etc.)	General process description	List of output	Internal and external process customers
	Transformed resources •One-off costs **Transforming resources** •One-off costs	Ongoing additional costs linked to the new process		

Savings due to improved resource utilization

Less material consumption (less raw materials)

Less machinery consumption (fewer machines needed)

Less man hours used (process automation and reduction of overwork)

Increased value for the end users

Output that is better designed for the customer in terms of design, flexibility etc.

Output that costs less to buy for the customers

Output that costs less to use for the customers

EXHIBIT 8.5 SIPOC Diagram Focusing on Costs and Benefits

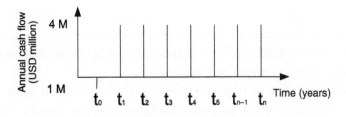

EXHIBIT 8.6 Cash Flows from the BA Initiative in the Radio Station Case Study

In the following, we'll be looking back at the radio station case study in Chapter 1, where we established that the BA project had implementation costs of $1 million, and then resulted in additional advertising revenue of $4 million per year. We shall assume that there are no ongoing additional costs related to the project, such as new employees and software. The risk-adjusted return requirement to the investment was set at 12% by the radio station's finance department. The cash flow from the radio station's BA initiative is illustrated in Exhibit 8.6.

The NPV of the project can now be calculated as follows:

$$\text{NPV} = \text{implementation costs} + \text{annual cash flow/return requirement}$$
$$\text{NPV} = (-1,000,000) + (4,000,000/0.12) = 32.3 \text{ M}$$

In our calculation, we assume that the $4 million is an endless annuity—something that could be questioned, of course. The completed business case shows that the project should be implemented, because the NPV is $32.3 million. Note that if the project were shown to be very risky, and the finance department therefore demanded a return of 500%, the NPV of the project would be $−0.2 million, and the project should not be implemented. This calculation is made by replacing the interest factor 0.12 with 5 in the previous calculation.

WHEN THE UNCERTAINTY IS TOO BIG

In practice, however, there are many cases in which it is very difficult to produce sound estimates of future cash flows for investment calculations in terms of revenue from BA projects. Cash flows related to costs are usually easier to calculate. Cash flows from investments in bond portfolios can be predicted or estimated with a high degree of certainty. However, if we invest in a dashboard for the management, with key performance indicators (KPIs) for the monitoring of sales processes, the financial implications can be complex or uncertain in terms of comparing and prioritizing projects.

We must then turn to cost/benefit analyses, which are built on arguments rather than exhibits. Such an analysis should indicate whether the project is viable for the organization in relation to its cost and risks.

A qualitative business case based on the cost/benefit method may consist of:

- A descriptive part
- The cost/benefit analysis itself

Let's assume that it was not possible to quantify the revenue-related consequences of the radio station case study, but possible to quantify only the cost-related ones. Then we can begin to develop the business case based on the cost/benefit method.

The Descriptive Part of the Cost/Benefit Analysis for the Business Case

In relation to the radio station example, the description could look like this:

Title: "Know the current listeners' preferences and adapt the broadcast to these."

Current status: The current status is that nothing targeted is done to adapt the radio production to current listeners' wishes. It's completely random which news is read and which music is played. DJs frequently attempt to estimate who their listeners are at different times of the day, but it's pure guesswork and not based on factual knowledge.

The consequences of not implementing: The radio station's production department cannot work in a targeted way to adapt processes to current listeners' preferences with a view to improving the "Average listening time" KPI. The consequence is less than optimal advertising revenue and less than optimal return on equity. In other words, the radio station's production department is not fulfilling its potential and is therefore under-performing.

Critical success factors: Since it's the first time that a BA initiative is implemented in the production department, the operational decision makers' change readiness is critical to the success of the project. Another critical success factor is whether we succeed in collecting the desired data about our listeners' characteristics and preferences at different times of the day and that this data is of the right quality because it was obtained through a questionnaire on the radio station's website.

Target group: The radio station's production department is the target group of the BA initiative, which aims to increase average listening time.

Risk: As illustrated in Exhibit 8.7, the risk is associated with the data collection via the new data source and the electronic questionnaire as well as the operational decision makers' change readiness. Note from the exhibit that it is not considered likely that these events occur.

EXHIBIT 8.7   Risk Involved in the Radio Station's Case Study

Risks	Consequence	Likelihood of Event
It is uncertain whether the radio station will succeed in collecting the desired data about its listeners' characteristics and preferences at different times of the day in the right quality, via a questionnaire on the radio station's Internet portal. Note, however, that the radio station is budgeting with advertising jobs from sponsors to motivate listeners to fill in the questionnaire on a regular basis and in a qualitative way.	5	2
There is also uncertainty in terms of the operational decision makers' change readiness.	5	1

Consequence (what is the consequence if the risks of the project occur):

1 = No effect

2 = Minor delay

3 = Delay

4 = Considerable delay or drop in value

5 = Impossible to implement the project

Likelihood of event (what is the probability of the risk occurring):

1 = Very low probability

2 = Low probability

3 = Sometimes

4 = A good chance

5 = Almost certainly

The Cost/Benefit Analysis Used for the Business Case

The cost/benefit analysis of the project may consist of an assessment of the eight factors in Exhibit 8.8 before and after implementation. They have been plotted into a radar diagram with numbers between 1 and 4.

As illustrated by Exhibit 8.8, the BA project is expected to add strategic value to the radio station along with improved competitiveness, improved processes, increased knowledge, and significantly improved measurement of operational processes. An executive brief could therefore look as shown in Exhibit 8.9.

PROJECTS AS PART OF THE BIGGER PICTURE

In BA we have a rule of thumb that says: "Think big, start small, and deliver fast." This obviously means that we have to look at our projects as part of a bigger picture, and to this aim, maturity models are useful tools. As mentioned previously these models are a firm fixture in

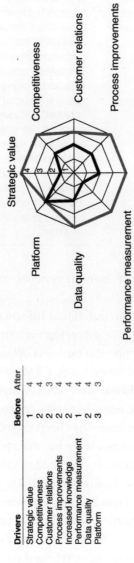

Drivers	Before	After
Strategic value	1	4
Competitiveness	2	4
Customer relations	2	3
Process improvements	2	4
Increased knowledge	2	4
Performance measurement	1	4
Data quality	2	4
Platform	3	3

EXHIBIT 8.8   Outline of Benefits

EXHIBIT 8.9 Cost/Benefit Analyses for the Business Case

Costs per Year including VAT	Benefits and Risks in Implementation
USD 1 million in the year of implementation. Subsequently, there will be only marginal maintenance and training costs related to the information system.	The BA project is expected to add strategic value to the radio station along with improved competitiveness, improved processes, increased knowledge and a significantly improved measurement of performance in terms of operational processes. Customer relations are also expected to be improved. Moreover, data quality is expected to be significantly improved, since we no longer have to guess who our listeners are. No benefits are added to the technological platform, and it therefore remains unchanged. Risk is associated with data collection and the operational decision makers' change readiness. It is, however, considered unlikely that any of the risk components will occur.

the business concept of most IT solution vendors, and they do have a number of advantages.

First, they are able to place individual information systems in a greater context (i.e., we can make a development strategy at the information system level and describe the business opportunities that they open). If we are talking about, for instance, CRM processes, it's difficult to generate campaigns if we do not have a data warehouse from which to draw information. It can be done, but with difficulty, and data quality often suffers. If a data warehouse has been established, we are able to design individualized campaigns, if we involve analytical competencies. The campaign will typically be of an added-sales or customer retention nature, where we are looking to optimize customer lifetime value. After we've established our information wheel, we want to try to optimize its effect by constantly optimizing the process via automation (which makes it cheaper), and by increasing the relevance of the messages we send our customers (more relevant content at a more relevant time), which is the idea behind "pervasive BA." In CRM, this is called *marketing automation*. The idea is that when a customer changes his or her address, for example, information is automatically sent to

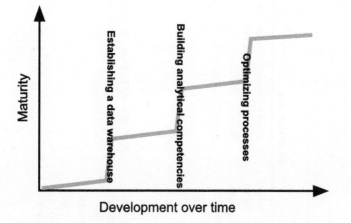

EXHIBIT 8.10 Revolutionary and Evolutionary Maturing of Information Systems

the customer about where to find the nearest local store in his or her new neighborhood. Or, if a customer usually buys a new phone around Christmas, we automatically send this customer a relevant offer, so that he or she does not even have the time to go check out our competitors.

This is illustrated in Exhibit 8.10, which gives a generic outline of what a maturity model might look like for an information system. As is also shown by the model, we use terms such as *revolutionary* and *evolutionary* developments of systems, where a revolutionary development takes place in connection with information systems being upgraded to a technically higher level. The evolutionary development takes place in connection with users of the technical solution learning to master it and internal processes being adapted to the new opportunities.

It is also inherent in the model that the development must take place in phases with each based on the previous one. For example, it doesn't make sense to implement a marketing automation system, if we do not have a data warehouse on which this system can base its actions and in which campaign responses can be collected. Similarly, it's quite difficult to carry out data mining, if we do not have a data warehouse, where the information with history is stored.

In Exhibit 8.11, we've made a table with the same four maturity levels that are presented in Exhibit 8.10. What we've done—true to

EXHIBIT 8.11 Generic Maturity Model for an Information System

Maturity Level	Focus Areas and Characteristics	Characteristics of the Information System	Processes	Competencies
4	■ Focus on optimizing the information system ■ Better and cheaper information and knowledge ■ Pervasive BA	■ Automated information systems that push information out to users	■ Lead and lag information accessible to both central and operational processes	■ Heavy competencies that can optimize processes base on strategic business and analytical insight
3	■ Focus and generating lead information ■ Masses of information, a lot of knowledge, and some automation	■ Analytical competencies that support a systematized generation of lead information ■ Automated distribution of lag information "on demand"	■ Central processes are supported by lead information ■ Most operational processes use lag information as decision support	■ Heavy analytical competencies with sound business insight

| 2 | Focus on generating lag information, much information, and some knowledge | Information is combined in a data warehouse
 Reporting systems established | Key people in the business have access to lag information
 Analysis are spending most of their time on generating lists and reports | Heavy data warehouse competencies with basic analytical knowledge |
| 1 | No focus on BA
 A lot of data and some information | Built on source data and fragmented information islands | Very few power users
 Difficult to access information
 Few analytical competencies | Varying IT competencies |

the principles of this book—is to divide the information system into technology, processes, and competencies and make a generic description of the levels.

The purpose of a maturity model for an information system is to be able to put it into a greater context, such as making a development strategy for the information system.

This also means, of course, that we can analyze which elements we need to be aware of in connection with the development of the information system by asking questions such as these: Do we have the people skills we need? Will the person responsible for CRM accept our going from a creative to a fact-based decision process in connection with the establishment of new loyalty campaigns? Do we have analysts with solid and relevant business insight to perform process optimization in connection with marketing automation, and so forth? A maturity model therefore gives us the opportunity to identify the critical success factors that we need to focus on to make sure that our technical investments deliver a positive return.

Finally, maturity models give us an opportunity to relate technical solutions to strategic requirements. If we want to increase our customers' loyalty based on historical customer behavior, then we will have to establish strong analytical competencies and, for example, a data mining solution. Moreover, we are able to, with a point of departure in the knowledge acquired about competitors' processes, gain an insight into which information systems they are using, and thereby how they use information as a strategic resource. In continuation of the strategic perspective, a maturity model also enables companies to consider where the market is going to be in five or ten years' time. If, for instance, we're feeling pretty sure that the industry we're in is characterized by everyone using marketing automation in the future as a cheap and effective means of creating loyalty, then the question is not whether we should invest in this solution. Because we obviously have to avoid losing customers, it's purely a question of when to invest. And consequently whether we want to be market leader in this field, or wait in the hope that the implementation costs will drop, and then make the investment, before we've lost too many customers by having CRM processes that are below market standards.

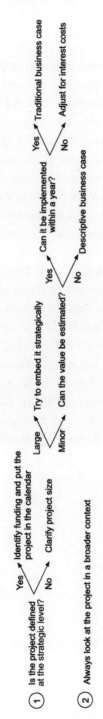

EXHIBIT 8.12 Chapter 8 Mind Map

SUMMARY

In this chapter, we've presented different approaches to prioritizing different project initiatives. Since there are quite a few things to take into consideration, we've made a decision tree for inspiration. (See Exhibit 8.12.) The tree also sums up what was covered in this chapter, namely that we always start by determining whether a given project is of a strategic nature. If the answer is yes, our project is based on strategic arguments, and should not be prioritized based on a business case. We must expect this prioritization to have happened at a strategic level. We should, however, make sure that the project has been given a budget and that we've got the full support of the business.

Over a considerable amount of time, large projects will take up a lot of resources, and we will therefore try to place them in a strategic context. If we don't succeed in this, we should consider whether these projects justify the potential opportunity costs involved, as they will reduce the agility of the BA function for a long time.

If we are able to come up with a reasonable estimate of the value creation of a project, this is to be preferred; otherwise we must make a qualitative assessment of the value of the project. And finally, whenever possible, carry out precise cash flow analyses the entire lifetime of the projects, and adjust capital costs, if they run over multiple years.

CHAPTER 9

Business Analytics in the Future

Business analytics will be everywhere, all the time.

Business analytics is not just moving fast, it's also in the process of developing from conventional BA to pervasive business analytics, which equips everyone in the organization and in the private sphere at all levels with real-time analyses, alerts, and feedback mechanisms. It's a paradigm shift with potentially huge advantages and far-reaching cultural significance. And it's happening already.

Instead of just measuring business results, after they've been achieved, which is the primary role of business analytics today, the next generation of pervasive business analytics will advise and drive the business forward with an arsenal of analyses and tools for real-time decision making. These will be delivered with a view to improving earning power and efficiency, and they will be delivered to people in all corners of the organization and even outside it.

Pervasive business analytics can be explained as omnipresent IT. And that means that IT will circle, inform, and advise everyone at all times, wherever people are. And we won't always realize when it's happening.

One example is General Motors' OnStar system. Here the typical GPS navigation system for cars is extended with an information and convenience service in a "pervasive" way. The customer service center at General Motors knows the real-time location of the car and can perform cross-reference searches in an underlying database to interesting places along the way such as hotels, restaurants, ad so forth. Would you like to be directed from your current position to the nearest cash point, airport, or a room at your preferred hotel chain? OnStar's underlying data warehouse has the information and can deliver this in real-time to your car as a service. And this scenario isn't even the future.

In the Introduction, we defined business analytics (BA) as: *Delivering the right decision support to the right people at the right time.* We believe this definition will continue to be true into the future and that BA will continue to develop on all three dimensions that are part of the concept.

As far as the delivery of the *right decision support* is concerned, there's hardly any doubt that the quality of the decision support delivered by BA will become increasingly complex and precise. We anticipate, for instance, that BA solutions will not just identify which customers are going to leave when and why, but that these solutions will also be suggesting the best way to enter into a dialogue with these customers. We expect that when a key performance indicator (KPI) is below its defined standard, the user will not only be alerted to this fact, but will also receive recommendations on what to do about it—preferably as early as when the system is forecasting foreseeable problems. Similarly, we anticipate that employees will be receiving not just emails in the course of their working day, but that these emails will be prioritized in relation to the tasks that must be performed on a given day.

With regard to the *right people*, we'll be seeing some major changes in the near future, to some extent because BA solutions must include users' preferred way of making decisions when information is distributed. Is it, for instance, a team of specialists who make decentralized decisions, or is it a consensus-driven decision culture surrounding the business process we're informing? An even more important trend will be that BA information will not only be supporting the optimization of business processes, but also be supporting the optimization of individual behavior in the organization. Employees thereby become business processes in themselves, since their behavior will now be the target for optimization. The previous example about when to read which emails illustrates this perfectly. If the local network registers that an employee arrives at his office and there's an important meeting in five minutes, the employee should be informed of important emails only. The rest must wait till the 20-minute break after the meeting. Similarly, a truck driver with an upcoming meal break may be advised about where to find a good place that serves well-made and healthful food at a reasonable price, so that he can stick to both his budget and his diet. Finally, let's imagine a busy businessman who, regardless of when he emerges from his meeting, is informed of which flight or train connection is the fastest in relation to his preferred way of traveling—allowing for the time he needs to buy a wedding anniversary bouquet for his wife on his way home. The ordering of ticket and flowers happens automatically, of course.

The third element in our definition of BA is the *right time*. Here we anticipate that BA solutions will increasingly send information to users whenever it's relevant, rather than storing information for when users choose to read the reports. This means that BA solutions in connection with the monitoring of business processes will be sending alerts to the people who are responsible the minute these processes deviate from their defined standards. The advantage of this form of real-time advice in terms of process deviations is that decision makers can focus on the processes that need correcting on short notice. However, this will reduce the waste represented by a process that is more or less run off the track and on the other hand, it delivers scope for possible savings in connection with the number of employees needed to monitor processes, since they no longer need to spend time looking out for problems. When problems need solving, the problems will go to the employees.

In the future, we'll therefore see the information wheel used not only for business processes, but also for the individuals in the organization, too, as illustrated by Exhibit 9.1. We'll also see information wheels turning faster—that is, the time between a new information need presenting itself and the delivery of new information will be reduced. It's perfectly realistic to imagine that every time a user accepts an action suggested by a BA solution, the underlying information

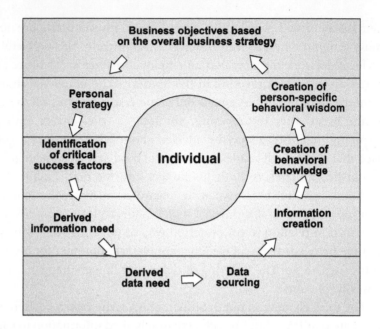

EXHIBIT 9.1 The Information Wheel with the Individual at Its Center

wheel will pick this up. Similarly, if a user dismisses information as irrelevant, this would mean the information is automatically downgraded accordingly in the information wheel. This scenario is actually not new; this is exactly the thinking behind the development of neural networks decades ago. *Neural networks* are self-learning systems, which continually adapt to the environment they're in, just like the human brain—thus the name. The new thing here is that the user of the network is not forced to sit next to a supercomputer, but can move about freely, and interactively train his or her own information wheel on dimensions such as preferred way of traveling, email behavior, meeting behavior, eating behavior, coffee behavior, leisure time behavior—dimensions that we imagine users to begin with might turn on and off, but that they will later have turned on all the time, because the information wheel efficiently supports and creates the user's lifestyle. This progression in thinking is on par with our use of the mobile phone, which we no longer turn off at night or when we're off work, even if we all used to swear that that's what we would be doing. Or even, for that matter, with our use of the automobile, which stank and was noisy and which my grandmother used to refuse the right to overtake her when she walked down the street, arguing that "the drivers of automobiles did not have the authorization to run her over." This the same vehicle that we now look at as an opportunity, which both creates and supports our contemporary lifestyle.

Just as the industrial era changed people's daily behavior, the information age will change ours. At first we will object, then hesitate, and then adopt the changes without noticing it. If you question this, just remember that a majority was opposed to building the Eiffel Tower in Paris. In the same way, the information age will offer us a freedom that we will feel uncomfortable with at first, but which we will come to adopt and allow to shape our lives.

You can buy books online on Amazon.com. If you inquire about books that have been discontinued or are not in stock, the system will suggest other books on the same topic, which might be of interest to you. The "pervasive" element is present here in the shape of an intelligent search and guidance as you navigate the Web site.

In the near future, you'll be on your way to the airport in a taxi. You'll receive an alert on your mobile phone saying that you will be late for your flight, but there is another departure at 8:20 PM with an available seat on Economy Flex. Do you want to be booked in? Alternatively, a train departing at 7:30 PM has one available seat on Business. Do you want to be booked in? The system recommends the train option at 7:30 PM, because it suits your profile as registered with the mobile phone company better. No doubt, some people will not like the idea of a future with IT information and guidance interfering with their lives all the time. Many might say that such a future is scary and will add stress to our everyday life. But is this true? Is it not less stressful to avoid arriving at the airport to find that you've missed your flight, than to be advised in advance and have time to change your travel plans?

A classic example of pervasive business analytics, which we may experience in the near future, is the computer HAL 9000 in Stanley Kubrick's film *2001: A Space Odyssey*. The intelligent computer sees everything, monitors everything, analyzes everything, and controls everything onboard the expedition and is "omnipresent." The astronauts are being fed with lead and lag information about potential problems and are advised on big as well as small things.

Pervasive business analytics now challenges BA systems with a demand on real-time data access to data warehouses and access from many different types of interfaces. In recent years, BA systems have moved toward Web interfaces or Web portal interfaces because of the need for global access. In the future, BA systems will be pushed further toward mobile entities such as handheld personal computers or mobile phones or something entirely different. If you need real-time information, these alternative gadgets become necessary interfaces, because we cannot guarantee that the user will always be sitting in front of a conventional personal computer with network access.

Real-time updated data warehouses at group level, also called enterprise data warehouses with service-oriented architectures (SOA), are not just possible; they already exist today in organizations around the world. It is increasingly acknowledged that business analytics initiatives must run on real-time data at the group level. It is often difficult to justify the investment to get BA up to speed, but it is essential for business users to have the latest information, preferably with a delay of zero seconds.

When the user interface changes, the real driver is the need for real-time information. And this need will always be there. People who are not interested in pervasive BA right now may still have time. But the inevitable development is taking place. We still have not seen one single consultancy firm in the world offering guidance on pervasive BA, and this could be due to the current limited market or due to customers' maturity, or rather lack thereof. However, the first companies are already out there on the cutting edge, and many will follow, if not all.

Referring to our information wheel in Chapter 7, the role of pervasive BA is, so to speak, to make all these wheels turn faster and smoother in a fully automated way as well as to deliver real-time information and knowledge at all levels in the organization. Many organizations are realizing that they have more or less the same products and services as their competitors, and it's increasingly difficult to create a unique competitive advantage via product differentiation. The final way of surviving is thus to squeeze the last drop out of the business's operational processes via improved decision making and, in this indirect way, to adopt a new kind of operational excellence strategy.

Obstacles to pervasive BA in individual organizations are that most major companies may have between 5 and 15 different BA solutions running. And often these solutions are nothing but a number of independent platforms and tools. This fragmented scenario makes it difficult for even expert users to learn about the many different tools. And what makes this challenge even bigger is that data is spread over so many source systems across the organization. So this is a matter of major data integration problems getting in the way.

The recognition is that everyone in the organization can improve their performance if they make decisions and act based on factual information rather than best guess, or how we did this last year. Historical data will be replaced by real-time data and predictions. The fragmented perspective will fade and be replaced by a more holistic perspective that stretches across the entire organization. We will move away from the static retrospective reporting results toward factual real-time information and analytical knowledge to drive individuals and business processes.

If you think this seems unrealistic, just try to imagine all the behavioral information that Internet sites like Facebook already have about their users.

It seems to us that the source data Facebook picks up is a tidbit for all businesses in the upcoming era of analytics.

Index